Marriage Spirituality

Marriage Spirituality

Ten Disciplines For Couples Who Love God

Paul Stevens

REGENT COLLEGE PUBLISHING
VANCOUVER, BRITISH COLUMBIA

Marriage Spirituality
Copyright ©1989 by Paul Stevens

Regent College Publishing is an imprint of the Regent College Bookstore
5800 University Boulevard, Vancouver, B.C. V6T 2E4 Canada

Printed On-Demand in the United States of America

Publication Data Cataloging-in-Publication Data

Stevens, R. Paul, 1937-
    Marriage spirituality: ten disciplines for couples who love God/
  by Paul Stevens.

        p. cm.

        Bibliography: p.
        1. Married people—Religious life. 2. Marriage—Religious
        aspects—Christianity. I. Title.

BV4596.M3S74   1997

ISBN 1-57383-088-7

Cover image licensed through Corel Professional Photo CD © 1995.

Gail,
My Spiritual Friend

Acknowledgments

Thanks to the following people for reading the manuscript and helping me craft this book: Roberta Hestenes, Michael Maudlin (my editor), Gerry Schoberg, Tony and Karen Bradford, and the students in my course Building Strong Marriages in the Local Church.

Two are better than one,
because they have a good return for their work:
If one falls down,
his friend can help him up.
But pity the man who falls
and has no one to help him up!
Also, if two lie down together, they will keep warm.
But how can one keep warm alone?
Though one may be overpowered,
two can defend themselves.
A cord of three strands is not quickly broken.

Ecclesiastes 4:9-12

Foreword

I welcome and rejoice in this long-needed book on spirituality in marriage. When my husband, John, and I were first married, we looked for resources to help us keep Christ at the center of our lives. We found little written to help us as a couple. During thirty years of marriage, I have been surprised at how seldom we have heard sermons or read materials that were honest about the issues and challenges faced by Christian couples who want to learn to pray together and live together as spiritual friends. In all the books on improving communication skills, dealing with conflict, handling mid-life crisis and yes, even on sex in marriage, there is usually little more than brief advice to Christian couples on the spiritual dimensions of their life together.

I used to think we were the only ones who were unsure about how to proceed. Now I know that many, if not most, Christian couples experience some uncertainty and confusion about the relationship between their spiritual lives and their marriage. In many marriages this is a source of frustration or conflict. It is a topic seldom discussed but of vital importance to healthy Christian marriages.

What does it mean to be Christian and married? Can husbands

and wives really be spiritual friends to each other? Are there spiritual disciplines that can help a marriage be centered in Christ? What is the place of reflection and action?

One constant temptation we have faced over the years has been to practice our faith by putting Christian activity at the center of our Christian identity and commitment. Involvement in church and other forms of Christian study and service are important, but they do not replace our need to love and worship God together as a married couple.

Now Paul Stevens has given us some real help in this most important aspect of life. He and Gail live out what is written about here. They are committed to Christ and to each other in Christ in a beautiful way. Their honesty and thoughtfulness make them helpers of many. This book does not answer all the questions; no book could. It is a very helpful resource for those serious about Christian discipleship within marriage. I commend it to you. May there be joy on the journey!

Roberta Hestenes
President
Eastern College,
St. Davids, Pennsylvania

Beginning the Journey

MY WIFE, GAIL, HAS HER HEAD ON MY LAP SLEEPING AS I try to write about spiritual friendship. I am thinking about the friendship Gail and I have built in our marriage, the challenges and rewards of knowing each other spiritually. We are on the upper deck of a Greek ferry traveling from one island to another on our twenty-fifth anniversary. My notebook is on my right leg and I am finding it very awkward to get my hand around her head to write these lines without waking her up.

Marriage is like that—incessant distractions from more important things. Being married can play havoc with your spiritual life. Many people feel that they were better friends in Christ before they got married. "Just when I feel that I am getting close to God," a friend says, "something happens in my marriage." Another complains, "I come home from a prayer meeting in seventh heaven and she informs me that the toilet is plugged." A tired homemaker sighs, "I'm just drifting off to sleep, my last thoughts about the goodness of God, and he reaches over to touch me. I know what this means!"

To be married means to have our privacy invaded, to live dangerously close to another sinner, to be interfered with by someone who claims to love us but does not always know how. Yet to be married also means to celebrate a sacrament every day, all day, through everything we share, even when we are not together. Yes, it is a risky business, but one that is fraught with joy.

There are many books on spirituality, and many about marriage. This book brings the two together, because marriage itself is a unique path to God. Unfortunately, writers on the contemplative life often act as if everyone were a monk, exploring the path of singleness, withdrawing from the world and enjoying what they call a "spiritual marriage" with God himself. But here we take a different journey. In this book we are about to explore the possibility of getting to God *through* our marriages.

"Would you be my spiritual friend?" I asked Gail this question with some trepidation. Choosing a complete stranger would have been easier. Christian conferees sharing a hot tub in an exotic hotel can let it all hang out, because when the conference is over they will never see each other again. Asking a friend would also be easier. Friends know us at many levels and are harder to deceive. But if they challenge us too much, we can opt out on the friendship. In choosing my wife as my spiritual friend I have chosen someone whom I am not permitted to leave and who knows me better than I know myself. A scary thought!

"But I'm not very spiritual!" Gail protested. I answered, "Neither am I!" But we concluded that it is sufficient that we both hunger for God and for a deeper relationship. We *are* spiritual enough.

Roadblocks

Yet even with our willingness to add this dimension to our marriage, there are barriers to spiritual friendship.

First, marriage has *too many agendas:* bills to be paid and argued over, bruised children's knees to be bandaged, an ailing car to be replaced, a vacation to be planned and garbage to be put out. How can we find the time or energy to pray together?

Second, married couples suffer from *overfamiliarity.* A group of friends in a small Bible study group may be inspired by my fresh spiritual breakthrough, but my spouse knows that the shaving brush still gets left out on the sink and my underwear on the floor. If she knows me this well, will anything I say seem novel to her?

Third, we have a *history of mutual sin and forgiveness* in our relationships. Not surprisingly, the Bible declares that sin first appeared in the relationship of the sexes. No one can hurt more pointedly than a spouse. Therefore the daily liturgy of husband and wife is something like this: "I have sinned against you. I am sorry. Please forgive me"—some of the hardest words to get out of our mouths. How can sinners in close quarters be spiritual friends?

Fourth, most couples have *unresolved problems* simmering on the back burner. Two persons so different and yet so similar cannot live together without producing some friction. He spends money foolishly; she seems uninterested in sex; the kids play one parent against the other; there is no energy left for talking at the end of the day. And the pot goes on simmering. It is tempting to want to wait until all the problems are solved before commencing a spiritual inner journey together.

Fifth, we are *afraid of intimacy.* Couples play hide-and-seek, Paul Tournier says, because "they fear that conversation, by becoming more real, will open wounds to which they are most sensitive, wounds made all the more painful, because they are inflicted by one's closest partner."[1] For instance, if I were to pray to God about my hurt feelings in the presence of my spouse, I recognize how real I must be, more real than I am in normal conversation where I have the power to persuade, to influence, to inflect my voice, to rationalize or to project my own feelings onto another. But if I fake it before the Searcher of all hearts, I damn myself to hellish hypocrisy.

Sixth, marriage has a *complicated structure.* Whether you have a traditional husband-over-wife hierarchy or a modern, mutual-submission, companionship model, Christians in marriage must distinguish between husband and wife—for God's sake as well as their own.[2] In this life we continue to travel from barricaded Eden to the idyllic New Jerusalem, but we encounter the effects of the curse throughout the journey (Gen 3:16-19). Every home is a political arena. The husband rules, the wife revolts and the kids get stuck in the middle. Sometimes it is the reverse. It is especially difficult if a husband thinks of himself as a spiritual director for his wife, or if a wife, misunderstanding submission, demands that her husband become the spiritual head of the home. Authoritarian hierarchies are hard enough without adding spiritual leadership to the definition. Fortunately spiritual friendship is not about dictatorship, as we shall see.

Earthy Spirituality

Each of the roadblocks to developing a marriage spirituality turns out in actuality to be a good reason to choose our spouses as spiritual friends.

Marriage does have *too many agendas.* But that means our spirituality must be exactly what Jesus intended, a matter of the whole life. The eye is good, he said, when the whole of one's body is full of light, when one's life is lived for God (Lk 11:34-36). The more agendas the better. That will save us from becoming religious. God wants us to have a spirituality which includes mowing the lawn and cleaning the bathroom, and which follows us when we are at work and when we are on vacation—not to mention while we are at church.

Overfamiliarity may be more imagined than real. How can one know a spouse too well? In a mature marriage spouses are still learning the basics about each other. A spiritual friend is someone to whom we can give an unedited version of our lives—a version our spouses know very well. Familiarity makes us develop an authentic spirituality that doesn't allow us to hide behind platitudes and pleasantries but penetrates the depths of our lives.

Spiritual friendship is not an intermission in life, but part of the drama itself. The actors in this drama are *sinners,* who, like Adam and Eve, try to hide that naked fact. Their sin and nakedness were revealed in the Garden, but God was the judge, not Adam or Eve. He took off their fig leaves of self-defense and supplied them with "garments of skin" (Gen 3:21). So today God takes away our self-righteous defenses and clothes us in his mantle of forgiveness, which is the foundation for true intimacy. No one can speak the truth more accurately, more helpfully or more lovingly than our spouse.

Marriage may not be a perpetual honeymoon but neither should it be a dreary trek. Spiritual friendship helps us work on *unresolved problems*. And if we cannot work on them now, we can at least hold them out in faith, like unanswered prayers, like the mystery of suffering. By faith we affirm the fact that we are married for good and refuse to bury the things we do not know how to solve. So spiritual friendship inspires hope and intimacy.

We are *afraid of intimacy* because it may be painful. But there is greater pain in the loneliness of keeping each other at a safe, comfortable distance. The movement of the spiritual life, as Henri Nouwen suggests, is from grasping loneliness to contented solitude, and from hostility to hospitality.[3] Marriage is not only parallel to our journey toward God but one of its main paths. As we cease demanding that our spouses fill the emptiness of our lives, we become free to be really present with them. And our hostility against them is transformed into the gift of welcoming them into our hearts where we can receive them freely. Loneliness and hostility are replaced with growing intimacy.

Marriage does have a *complicated structure*. Following Christ does not automatically eliminate politics from the home but it can provide a different context. Even a traditional hierarchical husband is a "safe" spiritual friend if he serves his wife as Christ served the church (Eph 5:25). No wife need fear the power of a husband who will wash her feet and love her to death.

A Down-to-Earth Sacrament
Instead of looking for God in the obviously sacred, I am inviting you to seek him at home. Marriage itself is a source of spiritual renewal because it offers three gifts to the spiritual life: sustenance, healing and growth.[4] Renewal movements try to bring re-

newal to marriages but seldom recognize that Christian marriage itself is a source of renewal.

The sacramental view of life opens us up to experience a spiritual grace like sustenance in the context of a down-to-earth reality. Take my sweater, for instance. Gail knitted me a beautiful red sweater during time squeezed from her busy schedule, time stolen from other people who need her. But I accidentally left it at a conference center. By the time I contacted them, it had been given away to the poor. Some lucky man did not know he was wearing a sacrament. Without a word Gail sat down and knitted me an exact replica of the first. But this one communicated "I really love you" with every stitch. Could God show me his love more directly than through acts like these, through my nearest and dearest neighbor? *Sustenance* is received from God daily in marriage through mutual provision of shelter, food, and psychological and emotional support.

Healing is received when anxieties and fears are dispelled by mutual acceptance and companionship. While daily ministries to one another can quickly be taken for granted, a period of stress often reveals that they are nothing less than a means of grace. For instance, my first day on the job as a carpenter pushed me off the stress scale. I could not keep up with my younger co-laborers. I banged my thumb with the hammer and, while walking along some floor joists, slipped down with one leg on each side! But when I went home that night, Gail ministered to me with a good warm meal, words of encouragement and a listening ear. When we collapsed into each other's arms that evening on the sofa, I was renewed by a spiritual grace through acceptance and companionship. The preacher in the Old Testament said, "Pity the man who . . . has no one to help him up!" (Eccles 4:10). Could God have ministered to me in a more direct way than this? Perhaps the preacher was reflecting on the sacramental presence of God in a marriage covenant when he said, "A cord of three strands is not quickly broken" (Eccles 4:12).

Growth comes through the discipline of adjusting your life to another from whom you can never hide. Because I know Gail loves me almost unconditionally, I can trust her hardest words to me, knowing that confrontation is not rejection but an opportunity to grow. She knows that I find it hard to give up opportunities or ministry situations that have passed on to others, sometimes with my public support but my private reservation. She says to me, "I feel that you are giving your colleagues a double message. You are saying that you feel hurt that you are not doing it, but you also say you want someone else to do it. I am having trouble knowing how to encourage you." When Gail confronts me this way, she is giving me an opportunity to grow. It is one of God's direct ways of helping me mature, a spiritual grace mediated through a very earthy situation.

Marriage turns out to be a school of Christian character, very earthy and very heavenly at the same time. It is a place to find God. Writing in the eighteenth century, William Law observed "that there is not one command in all the Gospel for public worship . . . whereas that religion or devotion which is to govern the ordinary actions of our life is to be found in almost every verse of Scripture."[5] The vows we took in marriage are reality statements: for better, for worse, for richer, for poorer, in sickness and in health, until death do us part.

God is especially present where the marriage is human, earthy, fleshly, vulnerable, painful, troubled and just plain hard. God is also present in moments of hilarious joy or deep companionship—

deepening and sanctifying these moments. Dolores Leckey suggests that sexual intercourse, that most earthy of all parts of our lives together, is a truly sacramental ministry. "In the sacrament of the eucharist we are offered consecrated bread and wine to eat and drink, an act of spiritual nourishment. In marriage, sexual intercourse is the primary (though certainly not the only) ritual of the sacrament. It is the extension and fulfillment of the partner's ministry to each other begun during the public statement of the vows."[6] All married Christians are ordained by God to a priestly ministry to their spouses!

Marriage Spirituality

Marriage spirituality is simply being intentional about the development of our relationship with God through Christ as a response to his grace throughout our lives.[7] Disciplines are not paths of spiritual accomplishment by which human beings reach God. Rather, they are ways of breaking down the barriers which keep us from being found by the seeking Father.

In this book I propose ten ways of breaking down the walls—together. Probably no couple will use them all, but no couple will use any unless they decide that it is worth trying. All of these disciplines will require effort: prayer; guided conversation as a way of deepening spiritual friendship; sabbath keeping—the discipline of worship and play; a retreat for shared solitude; study, to hear God's word together; service, to share full partnership in ministry; sexual fasting—the only specific marital discipline mentioned in the New Testament; obedience—doing God's will together; confession, the cleansing discipline; and mutual submission, the way to make marriage a daily prayer.

Marriage disciplines require such mundane commitments as,

"Let's keep Tuesday nights from eight to nine free for our spiritual conversation after the children have been put down for the night." If my spiritual friend were not my spouse, almost nothing would interfere with that appointment. But it takes unplugging the phone, arranging a baby sitter and sometimes a gracious conspiracy for two married people to share their lives in Christ. But when the effort is made, a couple discovers that God is seeking them even more than they are seeking God.

How to Use This Book for All It's Worth
1. You can use this book as the basis of a ten-week experiment in spiritual friendship as a couple. Set aside one hour each week and put it in your date book. Read one chapter at a time. Discuss it. At the end of each chapter is a short exercise or Bible study on a biblical couple whose experience illustrates the principle of the chapter. Couples can read the passage and use the questions as guides for conversation and meditation.

2. This guide can be used as a small-group study manual for marriage enrichment. Two or three couples can meet weekly for an agreed period of time (ten weeks) and use this guide as a manual. When you invite people, be completely honest about what they can expect to happen in the group. Some people find it very threatening to come to a group where they think the personal side of their marital life will be exposed. Make sure that you can honestly say that no one will share anything they do not wish to, or without the permission of their spouse.

3. A Sunday-school class or adult elective in the Christian education program at your church may use this book as a text for a course in spiritual friendship in marriage.

4. A weekend retreat for couples can use this book as a guide

and manual toward enriching spiritual friendship in marriage.

5. A series of sermons can be preached from the Scriptures cited and materials used in this book.

How *Not* to Use This Book

Sometimes one spouse reads a new book on marriage, gets fired up and then imposes his or her expectations on an unsuspecting, unprepared and unwilling spouse. Enthusiasm quickly gets doused and the thwarted spouse is left with smoldering anger. Meanwhile the "unspiritual" spouse, who probably doesn't feel he or she needs such a book, ends up wishing the book had never been written. If only one spouse reads this book, its benefit is limited to that spouse alone. This book is meant to be a marital resource, not a marital weapon!

As we turn now to explore the dynamics of marriage spirituality, I am encouraged by the realism and hopefulness of the marriage covenant shown by Morton Kelsey, an author on the spiritual life: "For nearly forty years my wife, Barbara, and I have both been on our separate journeys. We have quite different needs and practices. Over the years we have found a way in which two very different people can share their journeys."[8] One could hardly hope for more.

PRAYER: SHARING A SPECIAL INTIMACY

1

D*WIGHT HERVEY SMALL TELLS THE STORY OF A YOUNG* couple that decided to start their marriage by kneeling beside their bed to pray, an obviously good thing to do. But this young man prayed, "For what we are about to receive may the Lord make us truly thankful." Undoubtedly, from that moment on, prayer together got harder instead of easier.

There are two kinds of problems with praying with a spouse— one kind if you *do* pray and another kind if you *don't*. Prayer should be as normal as breathing, but for married couples it is often difficult. In fact, most couples find it harder to pray after they are married, and some even say that their prayer lives seemed to die when they got married. So if you are finding it hard to pray, be assured—you are in very good company.

If You Do Pray

There are understandable reasons why couples that frequently or regularly pray together find that they encounter problems.

Prayer is personally disarming. It is an act of honesty. In a marriage this is particularly threatening because of the totalness of the relationship. Gene and Judith Tate O'Brien in *Couples Praying* (the only book for couples I have found on prayer) say this: "One of the unsettling things about marriage is that we are found out! Our spouses learn, first hand, that we are not perfect. Our morning breath is asphyxiating. We are moody. We pinch pennies. Our chests are too flat. We are untidy."[1] On retreats of short duration with people I will never see again, I can be completely candid. But to be completely candid before God in the presence of my spouse is risky business. Can I express my hopes and fears, my secret joys, my painful memories, the sins that hold such hateful fascination for me? No wonder many couples settle with being just reasonably content. The price of becoming vulnerable seems too high.

Couple prayer is relationally exposing. The true state of our relationship will be revealed. The O'Briens quote one such honest couple struggling with the implications of being naked and not ashamed in the Lord's presence: "The only time I feel awkward praying with David is when I'm not feeling good about myself or when there's tension between us. I hate to pray at those times because I know I'm going to have to be honest and then I'll be vulnerable and probably have to make some change. But we usually end up praying anyway, because, no matter what, I don't like not to pray."[2]

As with other dimensions of spiritual friendship, prayer presumes equality, mutual interdependence and thanksgiving for someone who is different. Where headship in a marriage is interpreted as rule, control or power, or where a wife's submission turns out to be compliance, then husband-wife prayer is severely hampered. A husband may subtly preach to his wife through prayer, or vice versa. A wife may criticize her husband's prayers as a way of eroding her husband's presumed superiority.

Prayer together may not be so much a *means* to a good marriage as a *result* of it. Perhaps this is what Peter meant when he suggested that hindered prayer may result from a poor marital relationship (1 Pet 3:7). When a husband does not dwell with his wife "considerately" ("according to knowledge" KJV) or when the wife undercuts her husband's integrity, the couple's prayers will be hindered. Scripture describes this malady. Experience validates it.

Prayer exposes the level of our intimacy. Women are sometimes afraid to pray because intimacy requires being cherished, considered important and feeling safe. Stated negatively this means not needing to fear rejection, not needing to fear failure and not needing to fear betrayal. If in place of this fundamental environment, there is bitterness, neglect and suspicion, then she cannot disclose herself.

Men fear intimacy when they feel they are not loved, not understood or not respected. In addition many men are afraid of confronting deep feelings in themselves which they may not be able to control in a masculine way. They may have an underlying bitterness toward their wives for failing them in some significant way;

or they may be struggling with guilt, especially if there is an unconfessed sin toward their wives. It is not surprising that both husbands and wives often transfer their intimacy needs to a same-sex prayer group outside the home, thus short-circuiting the will to work on the intimacy needs of their own marriage.

When I pray alone, without my spouse, I can delay dealing with the actual dynamics of our life together. I sometimes use my prayer as an attempt to legitimize my self-righteousness. Or I use private prayer to justify myself the other way, through self-abnegation: "I am the one who is always at fault." Self-hatred in this nonbiblical sense is the cloak of pride turned inside out. It leaves *me* in the center. But once I utter that self-justifying or self-crucifying word in the presence of my spouse, I am instantly disarmed. It is an exposure I often prefer to avoid.

Prayer is spiritual warfare. Spiritual problems can arise from several sources: physical factors (illness, fatigue, malnutrition), psychological factors, fallen human nature and direct Satanic attack. Richard Lovelace explains the complexity of the human condition that affects our prayerlessness:

> The structure of sin in the human personality is something far more complicated than the isolated acts and thoughts of deliberate disobedience commonly designated by the word. In its biblical definition, sin cannot be limited to isolated instances or patterns of wrongdoing; it is something much more akin to the psychological term *complex:* an organic network of compulsive attitudes, beliefs and behavior deeply rooted in our alienation from God.[3]

Paul uses the word *flesh* to describe this nonphysical dimension of human personality that dogs our steps as we seek God and the righteousness of his kingdom. We know what the good is, but cannot do it. Lovelace describes it as compulsory unbelief, "our voluntary darkness concerning God, ourselves, his relationship to the fallen world and his redemptive purpose."[4]

The world, the flesh and the devil all contrive to make our marriages prayerless. No wonder it is hard. And when they succeed in keeping us from it, we are faced with a different set of problems.

If You Do Not Pray

Beth and Bob were married twelve years ago in the church where they met—Spuzzim Center Baptist.[5] Bob has a good job with a construction company and Beth is a nurse in the local hospital. Both of them teach Sunday school and attend services faithfully. Neighbors think of them as "churchgoers," as good parents to their two preschoolers and as a happily married couple. But a new factor has entered into the dynamics of their marriage.

Beth was invited to a neighborhood Bible study group in Linda's home. While her work schedule made her attendance irregular, she found a much deeper experience of Christ on Wednesday mornings with a dozen or so ladies than Beth and Bob had found together in their church relationship. These ladies really prayed for their homes, their children and their husbands. If only she could pray with Bob like this.

If one spouse wants couple prayer and the other does not, there is a conflict of expectations. The spouse who wants to pray may be tempted to pressure and manipulate the less inclined spouse through a hundred subtle hints. Comparisons with other couples may drive a wedge between them. Hearing that Tom and Linda spend thirty minutes each morning praying for their family before the children wake may simultaneously excite Beth with a holy longing and fill Bob with dread. If it is raised often enough, or used as a marital weapon, it can become an unmentionable subject. For such a splendid resource as couple prayer to become a matter of contention is really demonic. "An enemy hath done this."

But the solution is not to browbeat the reluctant spouse. In his advice to wives Peter had unbelieving spouses in mind, but Christian couples should show the same sensitivity to each other. Peter spoke about winning one's spouse "without words" (1 Pet 3:1). Instead of preaching, the believing partner (in this case the one who believes in couple prayer) should win his or her spouse by loving silence, by radical respect and by creative submission. Pray about your spouse; pray for your spouse; but do not prey on your spouse!

Couples who do not pray together have missed a rich resource. Prayer together has a synergistic effect, just as two medicines taken together can have a multiplied impact. Today no one should be sullenly or blithely self-assured about the success of his or her marriage. Prayer together is one way of reducing the chances of a rift because both husband and wife are seeking that third strand that will keep their marital cord strong (Eccles 4:12).

Couples who do not pray together are missing an important level of intimacy. Tertullian's words from the second century tell us how blessed life together in Christ can become:

How shall we ever be able adequately to describe the happiness of that marriage which the church arranges, the Sacrament strengthens, upon which the blessing sets a seal, at which angels are present as witnesses, and to which the Father gives his consent? For not even on earth do children marry properly and legally without their father's permission. How beautiful, then, the marriage of two Christians, two who are one in hope, one in desire, one in the way of life they follow, one in the religion they practice. They are as brother and sister, both servants of the same Master. Nothing divides them either in flesh or spirit. They are, in very truth, "two in one flesh"; and where there is now one flesh there is also but one spirit. They pray together, they worship together, they fast together; instructing one another, encouraging one another, strengthening one another. Side by side they visit God's church and partake of God's Banquet; side by side they face difficulties and persecution, share their con-solations. . . . They need not be furtive about making the Sign of the Cross, not timorous in greeting the brethren, nor silent in asking a blessing of God.[6]

Such a glowing confession! And yet we do well to remember that no couple gets there in a day, a week or a year. Like every other level of intimacy in marriage, this one takes time and work. But it is worth it.

Whether You Do or Don't

If praying together has become an issue, or is about to because you are reading this book, there are three important scriptural princi-ples to bear in mind:

The Bible emphasizes praying for *your spouse but says nothing about praying* with *your spouse.* We may assume that when the believers were "devoted . . . to . . . fellowship . . . and to prayer" (Acts 2:42), this included spoken prayer together. Certainly this happened in Acts 4:23-30 where we have a recorded congregational prayer with such depth and thoughtful content that it suggests something close to a liturgical prayer. But these references to prayer together are sparse and not well defined.

What is clear is the repeated command and invitation to pray *for* other believers. If couples were to spend more time praying for each other, they would worry a lot less about whether they are actually praying *with* each other. It might even "happen," just as a physical embrace might happen at the end of a day when there have been many other exchanges of love. This spiritual intercourse, like its physical counterpart, is not so much an action to be accomplished as it is the natural result of a relationship.

Paul gives us a wonderful model of intercessory prayer in Ephesians which suggests several excellent prayers for our spouses: First, he prays *that they might know God better,* "that the eyes of your heart may be enlightened" (1:18).

Second, he prays *that they will experience greater dimensions of God's love,* to know how "wide and long and high and deep" it is (3:18). You can pray for your spouse in terms of all the dimensions of his or her life, that the love of Christ would overflow through him or her to work-mates, relatives, enemies and the particular powers of darkness your spouse encounters.

Third, he prays *that they will "know this love that surpasses knowledge"* (3:19). It is more important that your spouse experience God's love than your love. We were made with an infinite need to be loved and to love, a need which can only be fully met by our creator God. It cannot be met for your spouse by you alone, nor for you by him or her.

Fourth, Paul prays *that they may know experientially their relationship with the family of God.* A surprising phrase in Ephesians 1:18 is Christ's "glorious inheritance in the saints." Paul is making the remarkable point that what God has inherited is his people. We are his most precious possession. God is connected with his people and each believer is made a living member of Christ's body. No one can be a Christian alone, nor is a couple separate from the larger body of Christ. Whoever heard of a church of two people? No

PRAYER: SHARING A SPECIAL INTIMACY

PRAYER: SHARING A SPECIAL INTIMACY 33

wonder there are spiritual gifts missing from the body of Christ! No couple disconnected from the body can experience the full range of the church's life: gifting, worship, ministry and mission, as well as growth in Christ. We should pray that our spouses will relate well to the people of God.

Fifth, Paul prays *that they will know the power of God,* the same power that raised Jesus from the dead (Eph 1:19-20). In the context of Ephesians the prayer for empowerment is not exclusively focused on what could be called the spectacular ministries—the controversial gifts like tongues, healing, miracles, interpretations, visions. Paul is emphasizing the power not to conform to a secular lifestyle (2:11-22), power to confront the secular forces that inundate our lives and culture (3:8-10). We especially need the filling of the Holy Spirit to submit to each other in marriage (5:18, 21).

Perhaps that is the greatest sign and wonder in Ephesians—removing politics from the home. Praying for power for your spouse seems like a perfectly good thing as long as your spouse doesn't get more power than you. What keeps some marriages from growing spiritually is the tyranny of a misunderstood equality. Equality is not sameness. It is a wicked thing not to want your spouse to be more advanced spiritually than you in his or her specific way. I once heard a woman say that it takes a mature man to rejoice in his wife's achievements. At the time I thought it was a good line for someone else! But I soon found out it was for me. Gail was the first in our family to become involved in neighborhood evangelistic Bible studies. That was her first achievement. Then she took the plunge into an inner-healing ministry. At first supportive, I was also cautious. Perhaps I was a little jealous. But with the help of prayerful correction and spousal patience, I was soon reassured and excited about another of her achievements.

So the Bible places the emphasis on praying *for,* even more than praying *with* one's fellow believer. These are not mutually exclusive, but if you have to choose one, start with praying for your spouse. You need no one else's permission to do this. But there is a further scriptural principle to be accepted, whether or not you pray together.

Scripture teaches that any kind of prayer is important. The form a prayer takes is mostly a matter of choice. Long conversational prayers may be spiritually upbuilding, but the Bible says nothing about them. In fact, the scriptural preference is for short prayers, in contrast to the direction of spiritual guides throughout the centuries.

> Guard your steps when you go to the house of God. Go near to listen rather than to offer the sacrifice of fools, who do not know that they do wrong. Do not be quick with your mouth, do not be hasty in your heart to utter anything before God. God is in heaven and you are on earth, so let your words be few. (Eccles 5:1-2)

Richard Lovelace suggests that Jesus may have had this in mind when he counseled his disciples not to "keep on babbling like pagans" (Mt 6:7). Jesus is concerned "to avoid overloading the conscience of the beginner or the weak believer . . . and to fix our attention on God who hears and answers rather than on the mechanism of prayer."[7] One Puritan said, "It is better to pray briefly, but often."[8] Gene and Judith O'Brien quote one couple who said, "A lot of times our prayer seems really repetitious. But I've come to realize that our lives are repetitious."[9] Or as Richard Lovelace concludes, "Even bad prayer is better than no prayer."[10] And couple prayer is no exception. God is more interested in your praying than how well you pray. No one has prayed in the name of Jesus, whether alone or together, and had *nothing* happen!

Putting It into Practice

You and your spouse could make a beginning at praying together
by saying the Lord's Prayer together each evening before falling to
sleep, or at the beginning of the day (Mt 6:9-13). Simpler still is
the agreement to pray together silently. It may come as naturally
as these words: "Let's just lie together silently and pray before we
go to sleep tonight." A prayer book is a wonderful resource for
couples who are not accustomed to praying spontaneously. Often
these deep and insightful prayers will lead eventually to a few short
phrases of your own. Or you may feel ready to start with conversational prayer. The greatest reluctance about praying together is
the fear of being overheard. It takes an act of faith to be willing
to be honest in prayer, but with a God like ours, what have we to
lose? Pray silently or pray sentence prayers or pray a simple written
prayer. Pray any way you can, because the only way to learn to pray
is by praying.

At the beginning of the chapter I mentioned the young man who
said grace with his wife on their wedding night. A far better prayer
spoken by Tobias and Sarah in a similar situation is found in the
book of Tobit in the Apocrypha. It is often used as a nuptial prayer
and is a good one to start with.

You are blessed, O God of our fathers;
blessed, too, is your name
for ever and ever.
Let the heavens bless you
and all things you have made
for evermore.
It was you who created Adam,

you who created Eve his wife
to be his help and support;
and from these two the human race was born.
It was you who said,
"It is not good that the man should be alone;
let us make him a helpmate like himself."
And so I do not take my sister
for any lustful motive;
I do it in singleness of heart.
Be kind enough to have pity on her and on me
and bring us to old age together. (Tobit 8:5-7 Jerusalem Bible)[11]

CONVERSATION: LISTENING TO THE HEART

2

WE SAT TOGETHER ON THE COUCH MAKING A FRESH AT-
tempt at deepening our spiritual friendship. I curled up beside Gail
and pushed my toe gently into her side, without saying a word, as
though I felt the need to maintain physical contact while we explored something we had not talked about for a long, long time,
perhaps never. We were going to concentrate on getting to know
each other better *spiritually*.

To be spiritual friends you must be intentional. We have had to
plan ahead, unplug the phone, or arrange for a baby sitter to create

time and space to cultivate our marriage garden. We also find it helpful to be removed from our normal environment, either by taking a weekend retreat or by simply getting out of the house.

Like the devotional life generally, couple spirituality requires a series of new beginnings. Most couples have an understandable ambivalence toward deepening their intimacy. They both want it and fear it. They are eager and awkward at the same time. In very disturbed marriages this conflict is quite intense. But even in healthy marriages this two-way pull is present, and we need to be sure that our desire for psychological and spiritual closeness is greater than our desire to protect ourselves. Our marriage vows pledge us to be the primary resource person in our spouse's spiritual life. So we must make sure that we prevail over our own doublemindedness.

"When did you first experience the warm touch of God's love in your life?" As Gail asked me this, she felt as awkward as most people do when they read a prepared question (like the ones at the end of this chapter). But you must start somewhere. A structured start usually leads to a free-flowing conversation—eventually.

"I cannot remember having any awareness of God's presence before Christ found me at a youth camp when I was eighteen." As I said this, I recalled sitting in church as a boy week after week redeeming the "wasted" time by planning my next carpentry project. Gail's experience was the exact opposite.

"It was so different for me. I cannot remember when God was not a definite factor in my life. When I was four, I was raking leaves in our back yard with the wind blowing against me. I remember chiding God for being so inconsiderate: 'God, why do you make the wind blow against me when you know I am trying to rake the leaves?' But God was with us both, even before we knew he was seeking us."

Gail's comment inspired my next thought. "When I was very young, I would play hide-and-seek with the neighborhood kids in Toronto. But I was not very good at either hiding or seeking. Some of my friends were so good at hiding behind garages or in shrubs that the person who was 'it' never found them. At the end of the game, they came out of hiding—triumphant that they could not be found. But to be so poorly hidden that you were the first to be found meant that you had to be 'it' and find everyone else. I didn't want that either. So I tried to hide myself just the right amount, wanting to be found but not too soon! I'm not really great at either hiding or seeking."

Gail began to reflect on how my childhood experience was a parable of my spiritual journey. I wanted God a little, but I was not seeking him with all my heart. "But at the end of the game, you did not want to be declared unfindable," she said. "And our seeking Father is always 'it' and ever shall be." Gail was not trying to find the psychological reason for my behavior but to help me get in touch with the movement of God in my life. I began to share another way in which I was found by God.

"I was walking in the woods once when I was on a prayer retreat, and I asked God to show me something about myself I needed to know. I saw some young trees bending over with the weight of snow, a tall, straight Douglas Fir and a huge but rotten old stump. I was not any of these. Then I saw a tree that had once been used as a post for a barbed-wire fence. The wire had throttled the life of the tree as it grew, but the tree grew around it until one day the wire was cut off. All that remained now was the scar, the visible symbol that what once was bound was now free. I am like that tree," I reflected.

"You are not simply a person with an emotional scar, but a person with a constant reminder that you are a freed person in Christ." It is tempting in spiritual conversation to keep looking for the roots of a problem, a poor self-image or a childhood without affirmations, but Gail knows that a spiritual friend is committed to nurturing faith. She was trying to help me be centered on God.

When I talk about my spiritual journey, I am exposing my spirit, the real me. Because I am reluctant to do this, I find that I tend to edit myself. Like a hermit crab growing up in a borrowed shell, I tuck my head back in when there is someone else in sight. And like that crab, I feel as though I am getting squeezed out of progressively larger shells as I become more and more spiritually open. Therefore I need a gentle and a helpful listener, which Gail has learned to become.

Soul Intimacy

Developing couple conversation is not merely knowing what to say but knowing how to listen. We were created with two ears and one mouth, a fact of anatomy not often matched in conversation. We were designed to listen twice as hard as talk. Many couples find it helpful to take turns listening to each other for half an hour each, taking turns talking about the subjects suggested at the end of the chapter. Even couples who have good conversational skills may find their own listening and sharing ability enhanced by this. It is all too easy for conversation in marriage to become routine, superficial and habitually shallow. But we hunger for more.

Sometimes soul intimacy seems to come more easily with a stranger we have never seen before and may never see again. The masks come off when there is no history and probably no future. Secret frustrations, secret fears and secret joys all tumble out. It is so easy because there is no accountability. But without accountability there is no lasting depth.

As I sit beside my wife on a plane, we are silent not because all is said nor even because this is the wrong moment to talk. On the other side of me is a woman with whom I could this moment have an intimate conversation. I could open up my heart to this stranger because it is safe; she does not know me and never will. Perhaps because it is risky, talking with her is an attractive prospect. With every stranger there is implicitly an adventure to be experienced.

On the video screen overhead, as we fly thirty thousand feet above our great land, there is a movie under way about a man and a woman meeting each other on a commuter train, as I might meet this stranger by my side. They "clicked," not just in romance but in friendship, friendship which neither of them had with their spouses at home. This movie is seducing me to think that I owe it to myself to get friendship where I can.

I have a choice to make every day of my married life. But really it is an affirmation of the choice I made on my wedding day. I decided then that friendship would not be the search for a friend with whom I could find intimacy, but rather that I would *be* intimate with the friend I have chosen. Like a monastic, I live a vowed life. I am happily bound to my wife beside me. When I do not feel like keeping the vows, the vows keep me. So I reach out my hand to touch Gail. She is sleeping now, oblivious to my thoughts, but not oblivious to the message on the screen. For she too made a decision twenty-five years ago that our soul friendship would be deep and lasting, not fleeting.

But there are difficulties in seeking soul intimacy with your marriage partner. Tilden Edwards, for instance, has concluded that the marriage relationship is probably too complicated to be an

arena for mutual spiritual direction. He encourages finding a friend
or guide outside the marriage and letting the fruits of this relationship enrich the marriage by enriching the partners.[1] It is an excellent thing not only for each spouse to have an "outside" spiritual
friend, but for each couple to have a spiritual friendship with
another couple. This can reduce the pressure on the marriage
relationship to meet all of our spiritual needs. But, excellent as
these are, outside relationships must never become an alternative
to learning to listen to our spouse's heart.

Listening as Spiritual Friends

Once we are committed to seeking intimacy through spiritual conversation, we find that that is only half the battle. For it to work,
we need to learn how to listen.

The twelfth-century Cistercian monk Aelred of Rievaulx spoke of
this soul intimacy in his classic *Spiritual Friendship*. While he
wrote his work in the context of monastic friendship, his thoughts
have a direct application to marriage. Aelred says that friendship
in Christ is a direct path to God, not a diversion from God. He
boldly paraphrases 1 John 4:16: "God is friendship, and whoever
abides in friendship abides in God." His thoughts about friendship
have great relevance to married friends desiring a deeper relationship through spiritual conversation.

Aelred describes the most elementary friendship as *functional*,
where two people share a common interest. There is little listening
to the heart in this because each listens only to find resonance for
his or her own personal interest. For example, I might delight to
hear that as a young teen-ager Gail taught Sunday school in a
downtown mission in Hamilton, Ontario, because I too am interested in serving the disadvantaged. Instead of drawing out the

source of that service, and helping her deepen the stirring of her heart by God's love, I can shortchange spiritual conversation by responding in kind, by pointing out similar interests which I share—not a bad thing to do, but not the best.

Aelred defined a second kind of spiritual friendship as *receptive*. This relationship is formed between a director and a disciple, between a more mature and less mature believer. While this relationship is valuable in other circumstances, this form of friendship is fatal to spiritual conversation in marriage. The minute I think I am superior or more advanced, I stop listening to Gail's heart *as a spouse*. I might not say that I am more experienced but I may think it, and the message is sent nonverbally. A one-way relationship never works well in marriage. This dynamic must not exist in a covenant made between equals. Aelred describes a spiritual friend as someone "to whom you dare to speak on terms of equality as to another self, one to whom you need have no fear to confess your failings; one to whom you can unblushingly make known what progress you have made in the spiritual life; one to whom you can entrust all the secrets of your heart and before whom you can place all you plans."[2] How can one do this with a spouse who is listening as a superior rather than as an equal?

Listening to the heart means finding our common heart in God, not advancing my own reputation with my spouse. If I say to Gail, "Sometimes I wonder if I am a Christian after all," it does not help me to be told, as Gail would not, "I once had doubts like that too, but since I was filled with the Spirit they all vanished!" A listening friend joins us in going deeper than our doubts. Because Gail too struggles with doubts, she can take my side in doubting my own doubts.

This need for mutuality in marital conversation is especially crucial where one believer has been a Christian much longer. It is tempting for the "older" Christian to assume the posture of a director. Conversely, the "younger" Christian might habitually defer to the older. Both of these must be avoided not only because it prevents in-depth sharing but also because it is based on a lie. It is simply untrue that a new Christian has little to contribute to an older Christian, simply untrue that more years as a disciple qualifies one spouse to become an adviser. I have observed the good fruit of believers married to not-yet-Christians assuming an attitude of equality when they listen to their spouses, assuming that God is at work even before he is acknowledged. When believers risk sharing even the darkest struggles of their own souls, some unbelieving spouses have been won in this environment of equality. Differences in spiritual maturity of Christians are, by and large, minuscule.

Spiritual friends find an equal or make one! Aelred gives this advice: "Never therefore prefer yourself to your friend; but if you chance to find yourself the superior in those things . . . then do not hesitate to abase yourself before your friend, to give him your confidence, to praise him if he is shy and to confer upon him in inverse proportion to that warranted by his lowliness and poverty."[3] No one can effectively minister to a spouse who is unwilling to be ministered to. Therefore the attitude of the listener must be, "I too am on the same journey. It matters not whether I have been on this journey longer or shorter. We need each other to find the way."

Aelred's third level of friendship is much closer to the intended goal of spiritual conversation. *Reciprocal* friendship is where persons have become pilgrims together, taking off layers of masks and getting to transparency. When Gail and I engage in conversation, such as the one condensed at the beginning of the chapter, we may cover some of the same old ground. But because I know she wants to reciprocate, I usually end up saying more than I planned and make discoveries as I speak. Gail's listening attitude invites this self-disclosure.

All spiritual disciplines are intended to set us up to be surprised by God. And we are most likely to be surprised in couple conversation when the process of sharing is fully reciprocal.

When Gail shares some of her spiritual struggles and joys as a teen-ager serving poor people in Hess Street Mission, I feel free to share the spiritual significance of my growing up in a lovely home next to a one-room shack occupied by a single man and his ailing mother. My mother could not sit down to a hearty meal in our home without sending a large portion to Mrs. Jupp and Albert up the hill. With Gail I am free to discuss my mixed feelings about these errands of mercy I performed as the nightly courier. Even though I was not yet a Christian, God was beginning to sensitize me to my need of a relationship with the poor, not just to give but to receive. In sharing these things Gail and I are not merely sharing a common interest, as would functional friends, but we are reciprocating by uncovering layers of each other's lives together.

For Aelred the ultimate friendship is the *knitting of souls,* that act of supernatural grace by which one person is joined and knitted to the soul of another, as Jonathan was to David (1 Sam 18:1-4; 19:1-4; 20:17, 42; 23:16). This "spiritual kiss" comes only as the result of risking, testing, self-giving and, finally, receiving grace from God. The goal, according to Aelred, is that special intimacy of spirit, will and mind in which one experiences the threefold kiss: physical, spiritual and intellectual bonding.[4] When all three are united in a holy way, two persons have become one spirit in two bodies (Song 1:2; Ps 133:1). Married spiritual friends also share the unique relational dimension of being one flesh. Most people want this ultimate friendship fast and easily, like a machine-knit sweater that can be purchased in a store. But soul friendship is stitched by hand, and every thread is savored. Each level of friendship is enjoyed for itself, and spiritual conversations add stitches to the relationship which lead us eventually to a union of hearts. But this is not likely to happen unless we are *intentional* in our listening.

Equipping by Listening

The truth that every Christian is a minister is one of the most widely believed and least practiced biblical doctrines, especially in marriage. All of God's people are called to minister the things of God to one another and the world, but they need to be equipped. The priesthood of all believers means that we all can intercede to God for others and mediate the grace of God to others, a two-way ministry (1 Pet 2:9). Ministry is simply touching people for God, being a channel through which Christ continues his ministry on earth through his Spirit. We do not "have" a ministry like a possession, an ear for music or a skill in carpentry. It is derived from our real relationship with Christ who is the one who ministers through us. But ministry also derives from our relationship with other people. It must be drawn out, recognized, harmonized and evoked—in other words, "equipped." This is true for both the church (Eph 4:11-12) and the home. Listening is one way to equip each other's ministry.

One reason why we do not minister to each other is that we are too proud to admit we need our spouse's ministry, too self-reliant to say, "Will you please pray for me about this?" The one-person ministry in the local church finds its fatal counterpart in the one-minister marriage. Men especially seem to struggle with this. They have no trouble saying to their wives "I have need of thee" in the sexual arena, but when it comes to spiritual ministry they often signal, "I don't need you" (see 1 Cor 12:21). But when we say to each other, "I feel discouraged today. Will you please pray for me?" we are equipping by our words. Our listening creates the environment that is crucial for this process.

The Equipping Environment. Because we have no earlids, as we have eyelids, we have learned to tune out what we do not want to hear. Or we listen to each other with a preconceived agenda. We interrupt with what we think our friend is about to say, finishing their sentence. But true friends listen for the feeling and spirit behind the words, the longings and the disappointments. As keepers of our spouse's soul, we need to create an environment in which the state of their soul can be openly discussed: to challenge, to encourage, to work through difficult problems and to name what is false within us. With great care Gail has asked me, "Are you punishing the people who have hurt you? Are you willing to forgive them from your heart?" We feel free to be this direct with each other because we know that nothing can make one of us reject the other.

But soul-keeping is different from counseling. Talking about our spiritual lives inevitably exposes scars, hurts, unresolved problems and relational difficulties. In spiritual friendship we are always relating these to our spiritual pilgrimage. We do not focus on the root of the problem so much as the root of our lives: Jesus. Counseling is like weeding a garden, while soul-keeping is like cultivating one.

Equipping Your Spouse's Unique Spirituality. Some people fail to listen with equipping ears because they unconsciously reject a ministry that is different from their own. But each person has a unique gift and ministry, as well as a unique spirituality. It is spiritual imperialism to impose one's own experience or path on another, or to reject another's ministry because it is different. A true friend cooperates with another's temperament and unique path to God. Equipping is not reproducing your own ministry but releasing someone else's. In marriage this means that each spouse holds the keys for equipping the other. And we will only use those keys if we can honestly say, "I need you and I need your ministry." In this way we will be soul friends and will help our spouses open up their hearts to us and to God.

Equipping Your Spouse's Priesthood. The marriage service is a couple's ordination service to mutual priesthood in the home. A priest brings the needs and praises of people to God and the grace and love of God back to the people: a two-way ministry. Nowhere does the New Testament state that the husband is the solitary priest in the marriage or God's personal representative to the wife. The husband is not responsible to God for his wife's spirituality. Ironically, if he were, that would frustrate one of the most important ministries of a priest: to get people in touch with God for themselves. True New Testament priests do not want others to depend on them but on God.

Therefore we listen for how Christ is functioning as the bishop and overseer of our spouse's soul (1 Pet 2:25). We listen for evidence that our spouses are finding deep needs met not by us but by feeding on the Bread of Life for themselves. If we discern that our spouse's spirituality is becoming parasitically dependent on ours, listening as a priest means equipping our spouse to depend on the Lord. Couples with small children can equip each other by giving the gift of a period of childcare so that, one at a time, they may spend uninterrupted time alone with God. Our goal is not dependence on each other but mutual dependence on the Lord.

One of the exercises at the end of this chapter explores each partner's experience of guilt. How we listen to our spouse's response to this is crucial. Priests know that we have a God who atones. There is a cross in the heart of our God, a cross that deals finally with the effects of sin on God and human beings. Knowing that there has been atonement, priests can risk compassion when they see and hear about sin. They neither condemn nor condone. They do not condemn because they too are sinners declared righteous only through the blood of Christ. They do not condone because they know that the mercy of God does not waive righteousness.

As we are priests to each other in marriage, we have passion—*with* our spouse. Literally this is what *com*passion is. We bear our spouse to God and declare God's merciful passion to him or her. Christian spouses are cross-bearers, mutual cross-bearers. Priest-spouses evoke priesthood in their partners, calling forth compassion where they might otherwise condemn or condone. Usually one of these two inadequate responses to sin is a signal that we have not sufficiently dealt with our own sins, and a spouse who listens to the heart will discern this.

Putting It into Practice

Spiritual conversation is more of an art than a skill. Almost anyone can rattle off answers to a series of questions on the spiritual life. But learning to listen to the heart is a lifetime vocation, the vocation of being a spiritual friend and equipper. But why not make a start by using the following guidelines? As you do, remember to listen twice as hard as you talk. Also, these questions are only possible starting points. Feel free to explore the many paths these questions may lead to.

Some couples find it helpful to take turns answering these questions and listening to each other's responses.

■ Talk about your first experiences of the warmth of God's love in your life. Share some of the details of your spiritual journey since then. Talk about the most important encouragements to grow in the Spirit you've had along the way.

■ Share how each of you now experience closeness with God, and how, where and when you feel most distant from him.

■ Discuss what you are presently doing to open up your life to the seeking Father, what disciplines or patterns you are keeping. What hinders you from keeping these disciplines? What would help you now?

■ Consider what you sense God is saying to you and to your spouse now, what place God wants you to have with him now, and what you think God wants to do with each of you now.

■ Share with each other which of the three persons of the Trinity—Father, Son and Holy Spirit—you normally pray to. This can point out which parts of God's personhood you find easy to relate to, and which parts seem more distant or foreign.

■ Share some of the pictures you have of God. Are there certain key words, images and metaphors of God that help you to respond to him? Are there some you struggle with?

■ Apart from your marriage relationship, consider the most important relationships in your life. Talk about your spiritual desires for these people and about your patterns of praying for them. Do you have some sense of what God wants you to do about these relationships?

■ It is not easy to talk about guilt. But couples find it helpful to share these feelings. What do you feel most guilty about most often? What do you do with your guilt?

■ Looking back on your life, do you feel you have been treated fairly? In what ways yes, and in what ways no? How about now? How does this affect your relationship with God?

■ Are you content? If not, what sources of discontentment outside of yourself are you aware of? What inside sources are there? How does this affect your relationship with God? How can your relationship with God affect your discontentment?

■ Share with your spouse about the meaning of your life. How did you discover it? Gain it? Lose it? How has it changed over the years? How does your relationship with God help you discover or develop your purpose in living?

■ What about the future? What do you dream about being and doing in the years ahead? Can you share these dreams with God in order that they can be clarified and refined? What would you say now is your goal for your devotional life? How can your spouse help you move toward that?[5]

SABBATH: PLAYING HEAVEN TOGETHER

3

AM I FUN TO LIVE WITH?" I ASK GAIL. THOUGH I SOME-
times feel like a West Coast hedonist, the truth is that I am not
always fun to live with. Over the years the playfulness of courting
yielded to the responsibilities of earning a living and raising three
children. I am more sober and serious. Both Gail and I have felt
the weight of responsibilities and problems.

Yet as our love for God and for each other deepens, there has
also been a deepening experience of joy together. A sabbath rest
permeates our busy life together. Being a couple in Christ is like

putting on well-worn shoes and taking a long walk together hand in hand. Sabbath was meant to be like that, especially for an occasional workaholic like me.

One of the goals of the Christian life is to become children again, playing freely and spontaneously in the Father's presence. That is what the biblical sabbath is about, and why couples can profit from keeping sabbath together.

Sabbath helps us connect with the God who calls us. It is a time when God can free us from compulsive behavior and preoccupation with performance. Undoubtedly individuals need sabbath. But so do couples, especially when marriage itself has become work.

Holy Leisure

Of all the Ten Commandments, keeping the sabbath is the only one that can properly be called a spiritual discipline. It is crucial for our spiritual health.

Sabbath was intended to be the leisured but intentional experience of reflection on and celebration of the source and goal of our life on earth. Instead of promoting leisure, the Bible offers sabbath. There is a deep reason for this. What we look for in leisure, God gives us through sabbath. People work at idiot jobs producing objects that meet no human need in order to buy experiences that will make their lives meaningful and fun. But what the huge leisure industry offers is a pseudo-sabbath. It seduces us into believing that our avocations are more attractive than our vocations. But if we believe this, we find ourselves internally divided, stressed and restless.

Sabbath was designed to be a playful day. It is an opportunity to reflect leisurely on creation (Ex 20:11) and salvation (Deut 5:15). It is the climax of the week, a climax couples need to experience together. Significantly, in the creation story Adam and Eve were created on the sixth day, ready for rest on the seventh (Gen 2:2-3). Sabbath was their first experience of the world. A week later, in resting from gardening and community-building in paradise, Adam and Eve were "playing" God; they were imaging God in their creaturely selves. God also works and rests, and we imitate God in both as regents, his kingly representatives on earth. We honor him with our work *and* our play.

In the New Testament, the sabbath foreshadows the heavenly paradise where work and rest will be one glorious experience in the ultimate garden city, the New Jerusalem (Heb 4:1-11). Far from being a negative, life-denying day, sabbath is pure play for followers of Jesus. Just as children imitate their parents and "play house," believers imitate their heavenly Father by "playing heaven" on the sabbath.

For children, work and play are a single experience. Children at play are free from instrumentality, from having to be efficient, from gauging their results. The inner world of children at play is unhampered by any need to feel productive. They use their imaginations freely. Only through the dreadful process of growing up do children learn that persons should be defined by what they do, that work is more important than play, that relationships must "work," that even prayer must produce results.

Children ask their parents, "Will you play with me?" In one sense nothing is accomplished by such play, but in reality something crucial *is* achieved: parent and child mutually affirm that they enjoy and prize each other. Why should married persons not say to each other, "Will you play with me?" And why not do it as a spiritual discipline, as sabbath? Playing together is close to praying together.

The Myth of Quality Time

When couples work together they are expressing dominion over *matter*, over things, over the stuff of creation. They do this whether they are designing a new computer program to handle household accounts or hoeing the back garden. It is part of what it means to imitate God as regents on earth (Gen 1:28). But when couples celebrate sabbath, they are seeking to express dominion over *time*, a much harder task.

When we organize our time, we regard it as a resource to be managed, like soil or nuclear energy. Time management enables us to squeeze out of our busy week one more hour for our spouse. That is not a bad thing to do. But when we view time this way, we may find ourselves resenting God for giving us so little time or resenting our spouses for demanding a place in our schedules. We complain that each day has only twenty-four hours rather than twenty-five.

Keeping sabbath involves treating time as a *gift*. When we humbly receive time as a good gift from our Creator, God can then open every day, hour, minute and moment to the possibility of finding rest in Christ. The purpose of keeping one day a week or one hour a day especially for God, our spouse and our family is to set us up for redeeming all the time in our lives.

We often speak of *quality time*, as though a transcendent experience of time can be obtained by scheduling an hour with our spouse. Sometimes such scheduled hours are spent in icy silence or bored activity. And sometimes these scheduled times will be wonderful. But the idea that quality time can be scheduled is a myth. Time together may be of good quality when persons give *quantity time* to one another with an openness to God. It is a gift we can give each other, but it is a discipline as well. And like all disciplines, it takes pushing aside human obstacles to make us available to be surprised by the seeking Father.

In marriage the human obstacle which needs to be pushed aside is the compulsion to produce and perform. And sabbath is just what we need to counter that, for it reminds us of the quality of play. Play is what God intends for us to have in our lives individually and as a couple. The following are three suggestions for celebrating sabbath-play together.

Fun-Play

When Gail and I lead marriage enrichment weekends we start with one question and one rule. The question is, "How long has it been since you as a couple were away from the children overnight?" To our amazement, some couples tell us it has been more than seven years! The rule is that during the weekend, they are invited to accept the discipline of not speaking to each other about their children. Sometimes there is an embarrassed laughter because some couples have talked about little else for a long time, and this weekend will be a time of courting again.

Every couple needs time just to celebrate their marriage relationship. For some couples, going away occasionally to a special place for a weekend of fun together is as necessary as going to church. Our heavenly Father smiles when we play together like that. Play is not wrong or "secular" but rather, if given to God, holy.

On our twenty-fifth anniversary one of our married children wrote us when we were traveling and said this: "It was important for us to learn we weren't the only thing in your lives and that your love for each other was greater, as well as different, than your love for us. It was a hard lesson at first to learn, but as the time to leave came nearer and nearer—what freedom!"

For over sixteen years Gail and I have been building and improving our little country cabin. It has been fun-play for us, an expression of shared creativity—perhaps because the materials were largely those rescued from the beach or from the trash bin. When we are there together, we experience a delicious rest that we know comes from God. Some couples find their daily sabbath in a quiet cup of tea at the end of each day with no expectations for heavy conversation. Communion does not require talking, and sometimes there is a deep rest simply in being together as good companions. Each couple must "play heaven" in their own way!

Worship-Play

Sabbath is being liberated from the tyranny of productivity and performance to rediscover our identities through love. Worship is therefore an obvious way to keep the sabbath together. We don't worship for what *we* get out of it. That would bring our utilitarian work-ethic into worship. Ironically praise "works" precisely because it lifts us above our compulsion to make everything useful. It is mere enjoyment of God, nothing more, nothing less. C. S. Lewis once said that in commanding us to worship him, God is inviting us to enjoy him. Worship is play. It is like one child knocking on the door of another and saying, "Will you play with me today?"

St. Theresa of Avila spoke of the desire to be nothing more than a toy in the arms of the child Jesus, like a much-loved teddy bear. The toy is loved not for what it does but because of the joy it brings. One sure sign that we know what it means to be in Christ is that we dare to believe that by sheer grace we can bring joy to God. It is unthinkable that Christian couples would not want to bring that joy to God together. It is surely our highest privilege, to please God together in worship.

A fascinating research project explored the connection of marital quality and shared spiritual disciplines.[1] This study showed that while mere church attendance or attending worship services did little to improve marital intimacy, praying together and learning to commune with God together did. Whether the spiritual disciplines were a cause or a result of better marriages is not clear, but it can at least be affirmed that worshiping together is part of a growing Christian marriage.

Most couples will start by enjoying the worship of their local church, preferably side by side. But there is great benefit in being open to more intimate occasions of offering praise and adoration to God in small groups and as a couple. The birth of a baby or the provision of a new place to live are natural opportunities to lift our hearts together and adore our good God. Some couples start each day as a family singing a hymn or worship song. Even the most timid can sing along with recorded worship songs at home or as they drive together in the car. Some of my friends use a tongue or prayer-language as they worship together and they report that this playful expression of joy has deepened their life together. Persons more comfortable with the prayer book and written liturgies will find them a rich resource. Where there is a will, a way can be found.

Whichever way you choose to make a beginning, it will help to think of worship as "playing heaven." In heaven, matter and time are both gloriously redeemed. Therefore we will be occupied primarily with worship. Far from being dull and stereotyped, the worship pictured in Revelation 21—22 occurs in a place of exquisite beauty and is filled with creative experiences. Sight, sound and movement are all centered on Christ, the Lamb. All our worship on earth is like a grand rehearsal, worth doing for its own sake, but intended to prepare for a grander occasion. We are "playing heaven." Therefore asking your spouse to play is not substantially different from asking your spouse to pray.

Sex-Play

Sexual intercourse is to married life what sabbath is to work. It is a sacred pause that helps us make sense out of our marriage. Through sabbath we rediscover that our daily work is really work for God. Through the sexual embrace we remember that the details of our lives together are for love. In each case we return to the routine knowing why it's there.

I have been exploring marital sabbath as a way of releasing couples from the compulsion to produce and to perform. Sexual intimacy requires this freedom as well, and sex-play is one form of marital sabbath. As with all sabbath expressions, this too should be a form of play. It is precisely the demand to perform or the fear of performing inadequately that reduces sexual intercourse in many marriages to a boring ritual. It makes work out of it.

Western society has reduced sex to a technique, a learned skill. But the Bible presents it as a way for married adults to drop everything and play like children. Many couples who are struggling with an awkward or unsatisfying sexual relationship can be substantially helped by agreeing for a limited time to stop short of coitus and simply to enjoy foreplay instead. The Bible even has a word for this delightful part of a sexual embrace, *tsaq,* used in Genesis 26:8 to describe how Isaac caressed his wife Rebekah. The King James Version uses the word "sporting" to translate this, underscoring that it is play.

The Bible devotes a whole book to the celebration of sex-play between covenant-partners. While it may also be an illustration of Christ's love for the church, the Song of Songs was intended to express God's good gift of sex-play. The Song has been called an extended exposition of Adam's expectant joy when he first met Eve (Gen 2:23). Some Jewish rabbis understood this well and forbade men to read the book until they were forty. It was too exciting!

I have graciously forgotten the name of the older Christian who once told me that only a person with a dirty mind could interpret this book as anything other than an allegory of Christ's love for the church. Possibly the reverse is the truth: a dirty mind that fails to celebrate God's good gift of sex or a mind polluted with an unresolved sexual problem may drive some people to "spiritualize" the text rather than to take its plain sense.

The Song of Songs describes two people enjoying each other in every way. It has a dreamlike quality which appeals to the imagination; like children in play, the inner world and the outer world flow together and are not restricted by instrumentality but are connected by sheer enjoyment. It is pure romance. God is the only rightful observer of this and he says (if this is meant to represent the voice of God), "Eat, O friends, and drink; drink your fill, O lovers" (Song 5:1). God not only approves of romance, he invented it.

Dolores Leckey suggested that sexual intercourse is the ritual of the marriage covenant. She compared it to the communion bread and wine, physical elements through which we renew our promises to belong to God and revel in his promises never to forsake us.[2] Similarly in the privacy of our bedrooms we renew, reaffirm and deepen, in a very earthy and human way, as human as kneading bread and crushing grapes, the covenant-vows we made publicly. A marriage consummated once on the wedding night and never again will not survive. The ritual of the covenant needs to be repeated again and again, just like sabbath. We have short memories and need these powerful reminders.

I think that for a couple in love with God, intercourse itself can be a form of prayer because of its powerful symbolism. In entering and re-entering each other's bodies we commune at the highest human level. And since our bodies are not shells for the soul and spirit but expressions of our whole selves, we experience the intercourse of our persons (1 Cor 6:15-17). We move in and out of each other's lives. Intercourse is not the same as merger; two become one not by losing their identities and personhoods but by discovering a deeper corporate personhood through intimate communion with another. As such it is a powerful symbol of our relationship with God, a relationship which is mirrored in the communion of intercourse. Christ does not engulf us like a merger would, but he does live in us and we in him. The genius of Christian experience is not the loss of our identity in Christ, but fellowship.

The sexual embrace is innately personal. But at the same time it seems to take us beyond ourselves. It is not surprising then that as Western culture moves into the pure secularism of the post-Christian era, the sexual act should be almost exalted as an ultimate experience. It is regarded as an instant, repeatable, mystical experience. I believe it was Malcolm Muggeridge who said that eroticism is the mysticism of materialism. What else is there if you have nothing more than matter and flesh?

It is also not surprising that sexual intercourse with a cult prostitute has been advocated by many religions as an attempt to achieve mystical unity with the gods. The religious use of sex in many primitive religions is dangerously near the truth, but tragically far from it. They lose the playfulness of the sex act and turn it into work meant to influence the gods.

But in the Bible the marriage relationship is a kind of *prayer*. Husbands are called to love their wives as Christ loved the church (Eph 5:25); wives, to reverence their husbands as the Lord (Eph 5:22). Christ receives our ministry to our spouse and Christ ministers to us through our spouse. This is but one reason for describing marital sexual love as heaven-play.

A beautiful marriage is a hint of something greater. So is our present experience of Christ, like the tantalizing promise of a not-yet-consummated marriage. The apostle Paul said he had betrothed the Corinthians as a pure virgin to one groom, to Christ (2 Cor 11:2). In biblical times betrothal was presexual marriage. A couple was married in every way except physically; only divorce could break a betrothal (Mt 1:19).

Therefore our experience of Christ in this life is pictured as preparatory and incomplete. We do not yet know as we are known. We wait for our heavenly wedding day, that glorious day of consummation with the Lord which is described in Revelation. Far from saying that there is *no* marriage in heaven, as Jesus is commonly misunderstood to imply (Mt 22:30), our final destiny as believers is *all* marriage. Heaven is one constant wedding supper of the Lamb (Rev 19:9). In this sense the Song of Songs may be interpreted as a rich allegory of the love between Christ and his bride, the church.

Marriage is a window through which we spy out heaven, and our sabbath times together give us clearer windows still. The particular devotion of keeping sabbath in marriage through sexual intercourse anticipates the joyful union of our Lord and his people, which makes earthly marriage true play, heaven-play indeed.

We have explored three ways of celebrating a marital sabbath. Each is an attempt to put aside obstacles so that God can turn clock time into quality time. This gift is most likely to be given when two people are prepared to share *all* the time of their lives as they allow themselves to be open to God. Henri Nouwen says that "the spiritual life does not consist of any special thoughts, ideas, or feelings but is contained in the most simple ordinary experiences of everyday living."[3]

The New Testament uses the word *kairos* for those times fraught with hope, meaning, opportunity and eternal consequences, in contrast with *chronos,* which is more like linear time or clock time. Marriage spirituality is not so much having common devotions as it is presenting our whole day every day to God, offering our *chronos* in order that God may turn it into *kairos.* In this way our days are infused with sabbath rest. Madeleine L'Engle says that *kairos* is that real time that "breaks through *chronos* with a shock of joy, that time we do not recognize while we are experiencing it, but only afterwards."[4]

Putting It into Practice

As a spiritual discipline sabbath involves a planned time for "playing heaven." We will deal with this first. But sabbath also involves an attitude of openness to a gift which may be given any time. This will be the subject of our second suggested exercise. The apostle Paul said that some believers consider one day more sacred than the rest, while other believers consider every day to be the Lord's day (Rom 14:5). For the full celebration of sabbath both viewpoints seem to be important even in marriage.

Discussion Topics for Planning Sabbath If Sunday is your sabbath day, discuss as a couple how you spend it. Does it lead to rest or to frantic religious work? What can you do to create a day of rest once a week? What will have to change for you to be able to keep this sabbath day together?

Consider as a couple what you do for fun-play. Recall some experiences of play together that were special and contributed to a sense of heaven. What steps can you take to make sure that your life together will not be all work and no play?

Worship-play is a second way we considered sabbath. Recall some experience you have had of communion in the presence of God together. Tell each other what would be the best context for each of you to enjoy God together in an act of worship. Plan for and protect these times.

Sex-play is a third way to celebrate sabbath as a couple. Discuss the spiritual aspects of sexual love by sharing what aspects of your marital affection are most helpful in deepening your communion with each other and with God. What can you do to create times and places for unhurried sex-play? If there are barriers here that need to be removed, confess these to each other and plan how you want to deal with them.

A Meditation Celebrating the Time of Your Lives Sabbath is not only planned time for rest. It is also the transformation of ordinary time into time which is open to "a shock of joy," letting *chronos* be open to *kairos*. "Making the most of the time" (Eph 5:16 RSV) is not squeezing as much productivity as possible into the hours we have but deciding to live all the time of our lives in the presence of God. That makes sabbath an all-day, all-week discipline for couples. The following meditation is designed to help you develop an attitude of prayerful openness to the sacrament of each moment. It is better to do this meditation of walking through an ordinary day individually at one sitting. But you may want to share with your spouse, afterward, what you learned, what you desire, what you are praying for in your marriage. You would edify your spouse by sharing any discoveries you made of how ordinary time as husband and wife became holy time in the past.

1. *Waking.* Before you roll out of bed, take a moment to thank God that you enter this day belonging to two significant "others": your heavenly covenant partner and your spouse. This day you can celebrate covenant.

2. *Preparing for the Day.* Washing, dressing, tuning up. Instead of letting your mind churn with ideas of what you want to do and accomplish this day, turn your heart Godward briefly for your spouse. What will your spouse be doing this day? Who will he or she be meeting? What pressures and problems will your spouse encounter today? When will he or she most likely need your supporting prayers later in the day? Commit your spouse to God this day, thanking God that he goes before both of you into this new day.

3. *A Quiet Moment.* Most people need to develop a daily time of Bible reading and prayer. As you take a few moments to read God's Word and pray, thank God specifically for one of your spouse's gifts—perhaps his or her unique spirituality or way of relating to people or situations.

4. *Breakfast.* This might be a moment of ultimate family confusion. Think of how everyone's agenda for the day coincides and collides at this moment. Present your spouse and each member of your family to God as living sacrifices, praying that they will not be conformed to the world but transformed by the renewing of their minds (Rom 12:1-2).

5. *Work.* Let your mind go through some of the typical activities of your workday. Reflect on some of the pressures and challenges.

You are immersed now in the principalities and powers of this age. Go through this day as a well-loved covenant partner, belonging to God and another in an irrevocable covenant. You are loved and cherished. Do not let those around you force you to define yourself, and your identity, by your work. You are to be known by whom you are loved.

6. *Play.* Will you play today? If you have children, they will help you relearn the joy of play.[5] Can you imagine playing with your spouse today? Can you remember moments of such play? Give thanks for the childlikeness you already have.

7. *Rest.* Sabbath can happen when husband and wife collapse together on the sofa at the end of an impossible day, or share two cups of coffee, or take a family picnic, or put aside the wallpaper rolls and do nothing together, or pray together in bed reflecting on God's goodness that day. It can happen in the middle of work or intensive ministry as your spirit goes into "overdrive" when God is working through you. The key to experiencing rest is not so much scheduling it (for that treats time as a resource to be managed) but rather treating it as a gift and a grace. Welcome it. Accept it. When time is treated as a gift, and when thanksgiving seasons our experience of time, almost any moment has the potential for transcendence. Michael Quoist expresses this beautifully in the following poem:

Lord, I have time.
I have plenty of time.
All the time that you give me,
The years of my life,
The days of my years,
The hours of my days,
They are all mine.

Mine to fill, quietly, calmly.
But to fill completely, up to the brim,
To offer them to you, that of their insipid water
You may make a rich wine as you
Made once in Cana of Galilee.[6]

8. *Turning In.* God has accepted you and your lives together as an offering of praise to him. Thank him especially that there is no more direct way to him than living the common ventures of life for his glory with thankful hearts. Then you may begin to say with Paul, "I have learned the secret of being content" (Phil 4:12). You may also have made a significant step forward in making your spouse a soul friend and discovering that ordinary or *chronos* time can also be quality *kairos* time.

RETREAT: SHARING SOLITUDE

4

TOM AND CATHERINE WERE SUCCESSFUL IN THEIR CA-
reers but wanted a year to build their biblical and spiritual foundations, and so they decided to come to Regent College, where I
teach. After that year, they would decide either to return to their
secular careers living fully for God or go into professional ministry.
Like many of our students, they had sold everything to come and
now were faced with the question, "What next?" The answer was
something they did not yet agree on.

I encourage married students, as part of their academic program, to make a retreat together for the purpose of deepening their life together in the Spirit. It is an assignment for the course I teach entitled "Building Strong Marriages in the Local Church." For Tom and Catherine, I thought it would also bring them closer to a joint decision on their future plans. They have allowed me to share the journals from their retreat in order that others might be encouraged and empowered to take a similar plunge. As you read these journal excerpts, note the following important dimensions of couple retreats:

Tom and Catherine needed to make a complete break from their normal environment to gain the Lord's perspective on their future. They chose a weekend away on Vancouver Island. Gail and I sometimes go to the guest house of a local monastery.

Their retreat started with a measure of awkwardness. Couples must determine to survive this initial awkwardness before they can really move into deeper communion. Sometimes starting with prayer individually and separately permits a couple to gain perspective and center on God before being together.

While disarming, the experience of being stripped of the usual busyness did enable Tom and Catherine to become more real with each other. Henri Nouwen said, "Without solitude there can be no real people."[1] And without shared solitude there can be no real marriages. Many couples fear this reality and always go away with their children or other couples.

Tom and Catherine wisely concentrated on *gratitude.* As they thanked God together, they overcame discontentment and put their vocational decision into perspective.

Physical touch seemed a normal and upbuilding part of their retreat. Some couples find it helpful in times of extreme need to adopt the unpopular discipline of sexual fasting, a subject to be explored in a separate chapter. You will note that Tom and Catherine did fast during the week following the retreat.

The most important work was actually done after re-entry. Retreats of short duration are sometimes dangerous unless they are linked with disciplines for re-entering normal life with renewed perspective. Tom and Catherine planned for continuing their joint spiritual journey *while they were in an ideal environment.* And by keeping a journal, they were able to conserve the fruits of being found by God together.

Tom's Journal of the Retreat
We needed a project to work on together, especially one designed to build our own spiritual friendship. God began providing for this time alone. There was a break in my classes and a friend volunteered to stay with our children so that we could get away for a few days. It was during this time of planning to get away that a renewal and excitement began to penetrate our marriage. Time alone, just the two of us and God, to seek him in prayer and to draw nearer to him and each other. To get reacquainted spiritually, emotionally and physically—boy, what a retreat! We took the time and journeyed to Victoria in hopes of a truly renewing and refreshing time.

Riding the ferry over, our conversation seemed to be slow—just surface talk, nothing deep. Just holding hands and enjoying the beauty of God's creation was overwhelming. We had finished reading together *Marriage Spirituality* [the first draft of this book], and brought it along to reread and discuss certain sections. Much of our conversation as we drove around Victoria began from topics in the book.

We went to Butchart Gardens and spent the afternoon walking, holding hands and taking pictures of ourselves together in the various gardens. As we talked, our conversation moved deeper and deeper into the plan that God has for our lives. We shared where we were with him and where he was in relation to us. As we talked and shared our deep feelings about our circumstances, it became overwhelming to realize that God was so gracious to us even to allow us to be called his children. We then began to review our past as we laughed and cried on our walk through the gardens.

There were not many people in the garden that day as it was fall and preparations were being made for the winter days ahead. I felt that we, too, needed to be changing in our attitudes toward each other. We should only want to change as God wanted, not in the ways we wanted to change each other. It could and would only be through his molding, shaping and calling us to himself that we would be drawn into a deeper oneness and spiritual friendship.

Our conversation flowed from our personal relationships with each other to our relationships with God. It was a bit sensitive, almost as if we were just checking the water to see if the temperature was right, each seeking a response from the other as we shared about our thoughts and visions of God and our personal closeness to him. After testing each other's response we continued to probe each other for more of the other's feelings. We were making headway into an area of our personal lives which we had never before discussed due to the fear and pain which could result. As we were finishing our walk through the gardens, our conversation became lighter and we prepared to go to the bed-and-breakfast where we had decided to stay. It was an old, renovated home that was almost in the heart of town and was more than adequate for our needs.

We rested there for a while, forgetting that we had anything else in life to do but relax and draw near to God and each other. Oh, what a glorious nap! When we awoke we prayed together, thanking God for all that he had provided for us, for his loving us and providing this special time together. We also prayed that he would guide our thoughts and conversation.

We had dinner at a lovely restaurant, enjoying a good meal together, sitting side by side watching boats move in and out of the harbor. We were touching each other in a loving way and treating each other as if we were on our honeymoon. What a wonderful feeling, just knowing that God had given me this beautiful and wonderful woman to share the rest of my life with. I recalled it was he who brought us together. It must be *him* that we jointly seek and draw near to daily. I was so grateful to God for this relationship that I felt was just beginning to bloom and would soon blossom into a relationship of beauty, precious and pure in God's eyes. However, there must be water, fertilizer and rich soil for this marriage to unfold into the deep relationship and permanent blossom which will be everlasting in God's sight.

I had slipped a card under Catherine's napkin. I had bought the card, then written a poem in it as a token of my love for her. (A poem—my first! How giddy I felt!) She was surprised by the card and shocked by the poem, and it was apparent that this meant a lot to her as she smiled, squeezed my hand and kept reading it over and over.

We talked as we ate and continued to ask each other some difficult questions. "Where do you feel God wants us to go when we leave Regent?" I felt particularly sensitive to this question, as I still wasn't sure. Catherine, however, had a bit more defined answer in that she felt we would be in full-time ministry. Well, I didn't, and that ended that discussion temporarily.

We moved on to other thoughts concerning our children as we enjoyed the delicious meal and just took our time. After dinner we strolled through the town, by the harbor, and talked about the creation around us. How wonderful, powerful and gracious God is to allow us to be a part of his kingdom! How mighty God is to bless man with the abilities to create and dwell in cities! Yet with all of this around us we observed how needy a people we are. As we strolled together, we prayed holding each other's hands, and the strength of the power of the Holy Spirit that engulfed me at that point caused me to weep. How awesome our God really is to have placed Catherine and me in another country to study his Word and to really draw nearer to him and to each other!

We went to another restaurant for tea and coffee to warm up, as it was cool in the evening air as we strolled through the park and down the city streets. Our conversation again deepened as we talked about who and what was the most important relationship in our life. I stated that I felt that God was most important, and then Catherine and the children. It even surfaced that at times I put them in reverse order. So we discussed each one of these relationships and how they should be fitting in my life on an eternal basis. We agreed to seek God together. This was a commitment we would jointly seek to fulfill in the days of our lives ahead.

As the evening drew to a close, we felt a deep, intimate love and longed to express it. We walked to our room arm in arm. We held hands as we sat on our bed, thanked God for the day, confessed our failures and rejoiced at the successes that had and would come through his being the Lord of our lives and marriage.

Catherine's Journal: The Following Week

After a weekend in Victoria of talking, praying and reflection, Tom and I agreed to fast on Monday and seek God together. We never imagined the intensity that this week of fasting and prayer would hold. The week was difficult, stretching, emotionally charged, yet wonderfully liberating.

Monday morning began with our own daily quiet times, then our time of united prayer. Afternoon found us in deep conversation interspersed with argument regarding our future. We had asked God to remove any barriers to our communion with him and with one another, and this he began on Monday afternoon. He opened a badly festered yet discreetly hidden wound and gently drained the poison amidst our buckets of tears. The evening was a time of extending forgiveness to Tom and accepting forgiveness from God for the bitterness which I had harbored for several years.

Tuesday we reaffirmed one another. Then Wednesday brought another time of sensing a barrier. It was the first time I could vocalize my feelings of betrayal and anger toward Tom and God. I had gone on the retreat feeling that we would be moved into some type of full-time ministry when we left Regent. I believe that God planted this desire in my heart, and I was angry that nothing was happening. I was angry with Tom for closing his mind and heart to any such direction and for leading me to believe otherwise. I had been willing to give up all my material possessions in order to pursue preparation for ministry, and now I felt deceived. More prayer, and more buckets of tears. I had offered my possessions to God conditionally. I confessed and received forgiveness from God and Tom. Then Tom was able to confess his own close-mindedness, and we ended our day repentant and forgiven.

On Friday I went to receive prayer counseling from a godly woman. The experience was awesome. The Holy Spirit enabled me to give to Jesus some heavy burdens I had been needlessly carrying, and a significant healing occurred in my life. Jesus took the pain which I had nursed for a long time . . . the hurt that had been a barrier in my relationship with God and with Tom.

I was apprehensive about telling Tom of my healing experience. What would he think about my visual image of Christ taking my burdens one by one? When I got home and told him, he noticed a change in my heart and shared my excitement. Within a few days, he too would go for prayer counseling and a similar healing experience. This liberated us to commune more closely with God as one.

The Journey Continues

Catherine and Tom ended up working together in management consulting (being inspired by the example of Priscilla and Aquila who worked and ministered—see Acts 18:1-4, 26; 1 Cor 16:19). Since they were self-employed they found that they could devote significant time to other ministries.

But not all couples have to wait until they experience a crisis in decision making before they go on a retreat. Every marriage needs times and places to step outside the normal daily pressures to see things from a different perspective.

Putting It into Practice

There are four problems to be solved in order to undertake this discipline: time, place, cost and program.

Time. Most couples will have to plan weeks ahead to take even twenty-four hours away. Tom and Catherine took the study break in the college schedule as their golden opportunity. Gail and I found that spending two or three days away just before Christmas in the middle of the frantic busyness was a wonderful and important break. For several years our Christmas gift to each other was "time," and this last pre-Christmas break at a nice hotel was a precious way to redeem this gift. Where businesses have flex-time, couples can sometimes arrange for a retreat during the school week when their children are occupied in classes and baby-sitting is easier to accomplish.

Place. This is harder to arrange. Hotels abound, but they do not always provide a meditative environment. Most monasteries and convents have guests houses which make excellent retreat places for couples wanting to be in a prayerful environment. Often the brothers or sisters can be very helpful both in creating an atmosphere and in giving spiritual counseling. Tom and Catherine chose to make a short trip to another city where they stayed in a home offering bed and breakfast. Some couples exchange houses or share their country cabins. It would be a great ministry for a local church to provide a place where couples could go for a retreat of shared solitude. Some members who have country cabins or second homes could offer their resources to others who cannot afford to get away. This leads to the third hurdle—cost.

Cost. If couples teamed up in local churches they could care for one another's children in turn, enabling couples to eliminate the high cost of baby-sitting. Making homes available when people are on vacation is another way of making an inexpensive resource available. I am so convinced of the crucial importance of celebrating the marriage relationship as a spiritual discipline that I believe that couples with very limited resources should consider using some of their "tithe" for this practice. I even have a biblical precedent. Deuteronomy 14:24-26 explains that if people live far from Jerusalem, they may exchange the tithe of animals for silver which they carry to Jerusalem. Once at the Holy City they can use their tithe to buy "cattle, sheep, wine or other fermented drink, or any-thing you wish. Then you and your household shall eat there in the presence of the LORD your God and rejoice." In this case the tithe enabled the worshipers to celebrate the Lord's goodness as a family, though this was not to be an excuse for failing to support the Levite ministers who depended on the tithes for their living (14:27). Far from "robbing God" (Mal 3:8) by using tithe money for a couple retreat, I personally believe we "rob God" when we sacrifice the full celebration of our marriage before God in order to finance the rest of the Lord's work. A couple retreat is the Lord's work.

Program. Most couples, like Tom and Catherine, need to have an agenda when they undertake a retreat of shared solitude, espe-cially if they are uncomfortable with unstructured time. A simple plan gives focus and clarity to their purpose in seeking the Lord together. Tom and Catherine had an agenda based on their deci-sion-making needs.

When Gail and I conduct spiritual friendship weekends for cou-ples at our local monastery, we start very gently on Friday night with some positive sharing on spiritual friendship. What follows is a series of short presentations on themes like "Welcoming Your Spouse's Spirituality," presented by either ourselves or another couple. Each brief introductory session is followed by an hour of couple-communication time, using an outline like the one reflect-ed in the twenty questions that follow. It takes a complete weekend for us to move through all of these themes. We cover questions 1-3 Friday evening, questions 4-15 Saturday and questions 16-20 Sunday morning. Many couples find that spending an hour in-terceding alone for their spouse proves to be the most significant time in the weekend. We always end with the Lord's Supper, something which, as we will see, almost any believing couple could celebrate in the context of a private retreat. The questions we use on a group weekend could be used by a couple on a private retreat. Why not plan such a weekend using them? The questions could be answered by each spouse alone first. This could take a whole morning. Then you can share your answers with your spouse and pray about the most important things you learned. This whole book could be used as a guide for a couple retreat. As with all retreats, the value of these discoveries will only be conserved if you make a definite plan for following through on one thing.

On Being Spiritual Friends
1. I am thankful that what we have in common is . . .
2. The area I (not you) most need to work on in order to be a better friend is . . .
3. Together we can improve our friendship by . . .

Welcoming Your Spouse's Spirituality
4. The most significant area of difference in our spiritualities is . . .
5. One good thing that comes to us in marriage because we are so different is . . .
6. I would feel even more "welcomed" by you in the area of my walk with God if you . . .
7. Please pray for me to grow in . . .

Interceding for Your Spouse
8. Some suggestions for praying for your spouse:
    a. Pray about your spouse's answer to number seven.
    b. Spend fifteen minutes thanking God in detail for your spouse.
    c. Ask God to show you how he sees your spouse, complete in

Christ; then ask him to show you what must change in you to view him or her that way daily.

Praying Together

9. I feel most comfortable about praying with you when . . .

10. I believe we could make a beginning at praying together (or take a step forward) if . . .

11. The most difficult thing I have to overcome in order to pray freely with you is . . .

Healing the Past and the Present

12. The most significant experience in my life which affects our life together in Christ is . . .

13. I would like you to pray for healing in me in the following specific way . . .

Discerning the Will of God Together

14. I believe we have already experienced the Lord as our guide in the following way(s) . . .

15. Together we need to pray for God's further guidance in . . .

Serving God Together

16. We serve God together best in . . .

17. Christian service and ministry pose a hazard to our relationship in . . .

Living for the Glory of God Together

18. I want to glorify God in our marriage by . . .

19. Please help me to worship God by . . .

20. Let's worship God together when . . .

STUDY:
HEARING GOD
SPEAK TOGETHER

5

D ECIDING WHETHER TO SEE IS AS SIMPLE AS OPENING OR shutting our eyelids. In fact, it is easier for us just to leave our eyelids open. Therefore we see almost everything in our field of vision. But deciding whether to hear is a much more complex internal matter of the heart. Even with our ears "wide open" we filter out what we do not want to hear or change it to fit our expectations. We are conveniently deaf to sounds that challenge our pride and our fantasies.

Study is a discipline that can help us with this. When couples study together they not only expose themselves to the same content but they learn to attend to the voice of God and their spouse. In this chapter we will look at three ways in which to develop this discipline.

Shared Devotional Reading

Reading an inspiring book together can be a good marital resource. When the children were small, Gail used to do the ironing late Monday evenings. That time was a good opportunity for me to read a portion of a book we were working through together. Now that the children have grown up, other times are more appropriate. Even reading part of a chapter at a time is a great step forward for many couples.

Some of the books that make good shared reading are *My Utmost for His Highest* by Oswald Chambers; *The Practice of the Presence of God* by Brother Lawrence; *Life Together* by Dietrich Bonhoeffer; and a superb new book written by a Protestant on marital spirituality, Mike Mason's *The Mystery of Marriage* (Multnomah). Another excellent resource is *A Guide to Prayer for Ministers and Other Servants* by Reuben P. Job and Norman Shawchuck (Upper Room). This last book is especially useful for couples in professional ministry and contains a wealth of devotional material. A deep book for couples in Christian service is Henri Nouwen's *Creative Ministry* (Image), which links personal spirituality and public ministry. An easy-to-use prayer workbook with good scriptural resources, questions and thought-provoking quotations is Don Postema's *Space for God: The Study and Practice of Prayer and Spirituality* (Bible Way).

Even this book you are now reading could be read by a couple over ten weeks, one chapter each week. Finding the time is not always easy, but there are routine chores like ironing or washing the dishes that could be redeemed by turning them into couple times.

Appropriateness is something to bear in mind. When Gail was in labor delivering our second daughter, I chose to read to her (in the hospital labor room) a heavy passage on suffering in Dietrich Bonhoeffer's *The Cost of Discipleship*. She sighed and said, "Couldn't you have chosen something lighter for the occasion?"

Shared Bible Reading

It is impractical for most couples, especially during the child-rearing years, to practice this discipline of reading Scripture together on a daily basis. Some couples make a commendable effort to get up every morning before the children. Other couples integrate this with a mealtime family Bible reading. As an alternative, couples could read a portion of the Bible themselves and share some of the fruits of their Bible reading.

As a personal discipline, I have found the McCheyne's lectionary of the Bible the best Bible reading plan for myself.[1] Sadly I confess that I had completed my entire theological education without having read the Bible entirely through. By using this Bible reading plan, I now read through the Old Testament once a year, and the New Testament and Psalms twice a year. The advantage of this plan is that one reads consecutively in four parts of the Bible at the same time. Almost everyone gets stuck in Leviticus when they start reading from Genesis to Revelation. This plan exposes the reader more widely every day. In my experience, there is hardly a day when one of the four passages does not jump off the page. Sharing this reading once a week is a useful discipline. Some churches provide lectionaries of the Bible that also can be used by couples.

Shared Bible Study

The cardinal rule of communication is "Don't preach!" This is especially painful for preachers or preaching instructors like myself to hear. But it is a salutary correction. People learn best not what they are told but what they discover for themselves. Cathie Nicol, a senior leader in the Canadian InterVarsity work, once stood waiting for a bus and thought she would occupy herself with all the great sermons she had heard in her lifetime. Her mind went blank. But when she started recalling the discoveries she had made for herself in the Bible, the bus came and she could not stop the flood of rich memories. Most couples hear sermons together. But that is only one way of hearing God's word. Another way is to share the discovery of God's word through couple Bible study.

Several study guides are available, some designed especially for couples. Alice and Robert Fryling's *A Handbook for Married Couples* (IVP) covers most of the important subjects of married life, with some biblical references. The same can be said of Gene A. Getz's *The Measure of a Marriage* (Regal), which has, in addition, many questionnaires and multiple-choice questions, all related to real marriage issues. Charles R. Swindoll's *Strike the Original Match* (Multnomah) comes with a study guide designed for couples. This last is more thoroughly based on biblical teaching and covers forgiveness especially well. The only marriage study guide I have found that explores Scripture portions by means of discovery questions (that help you find what the text says, rather than prooftexting your opinions) is IVP's LifeGuide Bible Study *Marriage: God's Design for Intimacy* by James and Martha Reapsome. The Reapsomes cover selected Old and New Testament passages about God's marriage design.

The two couple studies included in this chapter take a different tack. We will be studying two examples of marriages in the Bible, learning what we can from flesh-and-blood case studies. Often the Bible communicates divine truth through stories of real people, sometimes stories which show us what not to do without even telling us.

It is easy to find a book on marriage for almost any need you have—sexual communication, better listening skills, the languages of love and conflict resolution. The shelves of bookstores groan with marriage books. But finding the right Bible study guide is more difficult. A little discussion together may help you focus on a special need you want to address and would help you choose the guide best suited for your needs. If you have no focused need, the Reapsome guide covers most of the themes with a clear scriptural basis. If nothing addresses your special interest or need, why not do your own Bible study on the theme you want to explore? Do your research independently. Then come together and share your findings.

Couples unaccustomed to studying together will especially appreciate the value of study guides. By emphasizing discovery Bible study, the differences in bibilical knowledge between two spouses gets leveled. If one of the two partners has had theological education, the temptation of preaching at or teaching one's spouse is almost irresistible. But this gets minimized when the focus is on "What does the text actually say? What does this text mean?" and "What does this text actually mean to us, as a couple?" Some couples may find writing their own study questions, or even preparing a study guide for their church, an opportunity to experience rich Bible study together. To do this they could study the passage on their own, separately, and then come together to share and research as a couple. The task of writing discussion questions will become an opportunity to hone the message of the passage and apply it to their own marriage. Sharing a Bible study with another couple (using one of the prepared guides) can be a good start, especially if it encourages couple study in preparation or following the small group experience. Upon hearing a counselor say that most couples come for marriage counseling five years too late, one couple in our church decided to help themselves and to reach their friends five years earlier! They agreed to spend every Thursday evening having a study together. But they also invited their neighbors and friends (both Christians and not-yet Christians) with these words, "Tim and I are going to spend each Thursday evening for the next eight weeks using a study guide to improve our marriage. If you would like to join us, we would love to have you in our home. We are going to be spending the night in study anyway!" Some joined them.

But who should lead? It is a tragic irony that, like couple prayer, this splendid resource could be complicated by domestic politics, by power struggles and by jealousy of our spouse's strengths and gifts. Later I will explore my conviction that the husband is not the spiritual head or sole priest of the home. I want to argue for fully shared spiritual leadership and mutual priesthood and ministry. A couple study is an ideal opportunity to begin experimenting with full partnership, rather than with the leader-and-assistant model. Take turns leading, or agree that while the more confident leader may begin, the less confident one will take the leadership later. Leading a group of two turns out to be more like a couple conversation, which is what it was meant to be. By prizing each other's contributions, you will make great strides in equipping each other's ministry. A study guide with good questions permits almost anyone to get into Bible study leadership because you simply read the questions designed to unpack a portion. This opens up sharing and application, the vital ingredients of marital growth. Why not try this discipline too? Some couples may find it easiest to start with shared devotional reading, then shared Bible reading and finally shared Bible study. I am offering a sample study of this last suggestion because it is the most demanding. For some it may be just the right place to start.

Bill and Elana decided to do a weekly Bible study using simple discussion questions like those in the following studies. They set Thursday night as their night and, having read the introduction (below) and the Scripture passage (Gen 2:4-20), they shared some discoveries together.

A Sample Couple Bible Study on Quality Time: Adam and Eve

The record of Adam and Eve in Genesis 1—3 takes us beyond culture into the paradise of God. This is what God intended. Therefore both Jesus and Paul refer to Genesis 2:24 as God's description of covenant marriage: "For this reason a man will leave his father and mother and be united to his wife, and they will become one flesh." But our study will focus on another facet of this rich story: on experiencing the presence of God all the time.

1. Read Genesis 2:4-20. This account pictures the male all alone in creation. How does God make himself known to Adam?

Bill commented that it must have been wonderful to start out their marriage as a sinless couple in a sinless paradise. Adam and Eve had the unbelievable advantage of talking to God directly. To this Elana quipped, "But they blew it anyway!"

2. Though God granted humanity with dominion over all the lesser

creatures (Gen 1:26-30), God creates in Adam a longing for a creature that would be his equal and his opposite—Eve. Adam's "at
last" or "this is now" is the first poem, the first act of worship in
the Bible (Gen 2:23). Why would the provision of this creature be
an occasion of God-pleasing worship and gratitude?

*Bill said that while he had often felt deeply grateful for the gift
of Elana, he needed this example of spontaneous worship. He
really was thankful for a partner with whom he could share everything. Elana wondered if he would remember this when he came
home to a frustrated and weepy Eve!*

3. Adam and Eve had no liturgy, no temple, no Scriptures, no
planned times for prayer. How would they be able to enjoy God
without the helps we find so necessary?

*Elana thought this question helped them probe a deep need. It
was all too easy to have a form of religion devoid of a vital daily
relationship with God. Bill suggested that deciding to start and end
each day with a short prayer would be a big help.*

4. Read Genesis 3:1-24. How did Satan's temptations keep the
couple from relating well with each other? What effect did it have
on their relationship as a couple before God? How did it affect their
marriage spirituality?

*After Elana read Genesis 3:1-24 aloud she commented on how
important it was to discover that Satan is actively working to keep
them from finding God in their daily relationship. Bill commented
that it helped him understand why he sometimes finds it hard to
encourage Elana's walk with God and to bear her up in prayer.*

5. How have you now learned to worship God together in the

common ventures of life? Think of how and when you might begin worshiping God this way.

Bill and Elana spent a long time discussing this question. Bill's background made a strong separation of the sacred and the secular. There was little connection between Sunday and Monday. He asked Elana to pray for him that he could do even little shared activities, like putting the children down at night, as an act of worship. Elana shared some needs in this area as well. They concluded that Adam and Eve are not only a picture of our "past," but Adam and Eve before their sin are a picture of the future into which we are moving in Christ.

Putting It into Practice

The next Bible study can be used as a guide for a couple study on some agreed evening. As you do this, you can expect to be surprised by the discoveries you make on your own.

A Couple Bible Study on Spiritual Disciplines: Samson and Delilah. Sometimes the Bible tells us what to do by giving us an example of what happens when we fail to do it. Samson's tragic marriage to Delilah is an illustration of this. Samson had a unique calling of God to be a Nazirite, one who was specially dedicated to God. His uncut hair was a symbol of this devotion. He was endowed with a strong body and a special anointing from the Holy Spirit. Samson was raised up by God at the time of the judges, before the nation was unified around a king. But the lack of shared spiritual disciplines in his marriage was his undoing.

1. Read Judges 16:4-22. By marrying outside the community of faith, Samson had already jeopardized any possibility of fellowship. What means does Delilah use to take advantage of Samson's spiritual secret?

2. When his hair had been shorn the Scripture says that Samson "did not know that the LORD had left him" (v. 20). In what kinds of situations might a couple think they still are in the Lord's will while being bereft of power and spiritual life? Is there a time when this has happened in your marriage?

3. Even though Samson was "out of God's will" in marrying a Philistine, the inspired historian comments that "this was from the LORD" (14:4) who wove Samson's decision into his purpose to free the Israelites from the tyranny of Philistia. Read Judges 16:23-31. What redeeming features in Samson are revealed in the closing moments of his life?

4. Discuss with your spouse how you might inadvertently sabotage each other's personal spiritual disciplines under the guise of wanting more love from each other (16:15). How can you be more direct about your own needs? How can you better support your spouse's spiritual growth?

SERVICE: FULL PARTNERSHIP IN MINISTRY

6

THE HUNGER FOR FELLOWSHIP WITHIN *MARRIAGE IS IN-*ternational and transcultural. African marriages are sometimes caricatured as "organic" and orientated to childbearing and survival tasks. But I asked some students I teach in Kenya to complete a questionnaire prioritizing how they wished to be loved by their spouses. I explained to them, "In North America we call this the languages of love, because with so many ways of communicating 'I love you' without words, it is important that husbands and wives communicate just how they need to be loved."

My African pastors in training, both men and women, listed the following two top priorities for receiving love from their spouses: "praying *with* my spouse about our lives" and "choosing Christian service that we can do together." These were even more important than the language of touch! But my questionnaire did unearth a serious problem.

"Walimu," they asked (this means "teacher" in Swahili, although my Kenyan students privately call me "the bald one" and Gail "the wife of the bald one"), "how is it possible for us to be pastors and at the same time be good husbands and wives and good parents?"

The kerosene lamps were lit and we talked far into the night about a crucial problem in the church of this great land. Older pastors had been taught that following Jesus in ministry meant "hating father, mother and wives." Most of them covered a wide area on foot or bicycle, often pastoring eight or ten churches. It was simply not possible to be home more than a night each week. Many left their families in one part of the country on their little *shamba* farms while the pastor ministered as a crosscultural missionary hundreds of miles away in another tribal area, returning home every three or four weeks. I have yet to meet anyone happy with the arrangement, but it is so universal that it is almost law for Christians in Africa.

"But you have been teaching us, Walimu, that serving God together is a path to God. How can we do that when we spend so much time apart?" A long discussion followed on the pragmatics of developing full partnership, matters which we will take up now. I am praying that the next generation of pastors in Kenya will be able to experience the discipline of a shared ministry.

Equality in Service

For married Christians, ministry should normally be shared. *When God calls a couple to serve, both must hear the call.* For one to capitulate to the other's call is wrong. If one hesitates, the other should wait. There is much that can be done while waiting.

Unfortunately, Sam was not sensitive to Sue's reservations. He believed that marriage is subordinate to ministry. And he felt called to serve overseas. Sue did not. Sam dragged his wife kicking and screaming into a male-dominated Islamic culture that was a source of further bitterness for her. At first, their children embraced their father's "sacrifice," which for Sue had felt more like a slaughter. But as the children grew up, they came to hate the God that had demanded such excruciating obedience from his loved ones. In trying to save the world, Sam lost his own family and began to wonder, in the end, what he had gained.

Jesus addressed this issue in the Jewish culture of his day. *Corban* was a popular practice where someone could technically dedicate their money to the Temple so that it would not have to be spent on supporting one's aging parents. Meanwhile, the money was available for personal use (Mk 7:6-13). Jesus said: "Thus you nullify the word of God." He could have just as easily used the example of sacrificing one's family for devoted service in the church or world. Both are sacrifices that Jesus never asked his children to make.

In *Spiritual Friendship,* Aelred of Rievaulx comments:
How beautiful it is that the second human being was taken from the side of the first, so that nature might teach that human beings are equal and, as it were, collateral, and there is in human affairs neither a superior nor an inferior, a characteristic of true friendship.[1]

We may understand Aelred's reference to Adam and Eve as applying to the equality of husband and wife in shared service.[2]

This is especially important for high-profile Christian leaders whose spouses often feel like sidekicks rather than full participating partners. When couples compete for the limelight, or one is jealous of the other's charisma or following, a reverse synergy sets in. Even their individual ministries are polluted. I am not suggesting that married servants of God must do everything together—that would be suffocating. But what they choose to do together must be something in which each feels fully needed. Where there are differences, as there will inevitably be, the more influential partner has the responsibility to *empower* the weaker one by affirming in public and private why they have chosen to serve together. There are deep reasons for this, as we will now explore.

Unfortunately the principle of equality is not universally accepted. C. S. Lewis argues that a male in a masculine uniform must give leadership to the church since God is masculine and the church, Christ's bride, is feminine. Thus only a male can represent God to the church.[3] But the argument is curiously reversible.

If males are needed to represent God to the church (a disputable point in itself), then only females can represent the church to God. Thus only females should give worship leadership to the church when the bride of Christ gives her offerings of praise and thanksgiving to God. And only female ministers should officiate at the Eucharist or Lord's Supper, the supreme act of corporate thanksgiving. Or so the argument would go.

But wouldn't it be far better to have men and women serving in full partnership, each contributing gender-uniqueness to the richness of shared ministry?

Personally I find the arguments that women are equal in dignity but subordinate in government and ministry quite unconvincing and demeaning of the complete work of Jesus under the new covenant.[4] Husbands and wives, like Aquila and Priscilla in the Bible study at the end of this chapter, serve God best as partners—not as leader and subordinate.

Sharing the leadership of a neighborhood Bible study, team-teaching a Sunday-school class or caring for a single-parent family on public assistance will have spin-off benefits for marriage spirituality. Spouses learn to prize each other in new ways. They learn interdependence. By concentrating on needs outside of the home, they can discover deeper levels of fellowship. But welcoming that interdependence of sexual spiritualities can be a complicated challenge for a couple to accept.

Welcoming Sexual Spiritualities
I cannot remember exactly when I first became interested in members of the opposite sex, but it was very early. In kindergarten I sat behind Mary, a delightful little girl with long, blonde pigtails that reached down to my desktop. One day we were given some scissors to cut paper, and as an early experiment in gaining a female's attention, I decided to cut off four inches of one of those big, blonde pigtails. I got Mary's *attention* right away, followed quickly by a *detention* from my teacher!

Subsequently I learned more socialized ways of celebrating the difference between the sexes. But the question we need to consider is whether the sexual differences we find so intriguing are also matched by spiritual differences. Are there masculine and feminine spiritualities?

This is a "fools rush in" issue. It would be easier to rely on those studies that conclude that all the nonphysical characteristics of men and women are culturally learned and not innate. After all, of the forty-six chromosomes in every fertilized egg, only two relate to our sexuality. It is well known that every man and every woman has both androgens (the male hormones) and estrogens (the female hormones) in varying proportions. Some studies suggest that society has stereotyped males as aggressive, independent, unemotional, logical, direct, adventuresome and ambitious; and the females as passive, emotional, dependent, less competitive, nonobjective, submissive, religious and in need of security.[5]

But for every such study there is another that suggests that there are innate differences between men and women, which might lead to unique spiritualities. Men and women are different and complementary not only in their bodies but in their psychologies and spiritualities. We do not *have* bodies as appendages of our persons. We *are* bodies; we *are* souls; we *are* spirits. We are integrated wholes. Therefore our sexual differences are more than physical. But trying to define that difference is another matter.

Kierkegaard dared to suggest that a woman's femininity is expressed primarily in her devotedness.[6] Does this perhaps explain why women more than men seem to be attracted to the average church service? Or have we simply presented the faith in a way that does not capture aggressive and action-oriented men?

When Henri Nouwen entered a Trappist monastery for seven months, he had to come to grips with the sexuality of his spirituality.

John Eudes (the abbot) . . . made me see how masculine my emotional life really is, how competition and rivalry are central to my inner life, and how underdeveloped my feminine side has remained. He told me about St. Bernard who didn't hesitate to call the task of the monk a woman's task (compared with the virile task of the secular priest) and to remind the abbot (the word comes from abba-father) of his motherly responsibilities.[7]

Reflecting on the place of Mary in the Roman Catholic tradition, Nouwen comments that "Mary helps me to come in touch again with my receptive, contemplative side to counterbalance my one-sided aggressive, hostile, domineering, competitive side."[8]

An article by Nor Hall in *The Westminster Dictionary of Christian Spirituality* explores the principle that our response to Christ is conditioned by our sexuality.

> The feminine experience of God is distinct but not separate from the masculine experience. . . . Each calls forth in the other essential elements of response to Christ. . . . The bodily experience of a woman is intrinsic to understanding her response to the divine. Biologically a woman is determined by her role as bearer and deliverer of life. Thus, her entire life is a preparation for the birthing experience and the subsequent nurturing of the life to which she has given birth. There is no woman, whether she has actually given birth or not, whose psyche, soul and spirit remain outside the influence of these bodily imperatives.[9]

I once heard a woman from Uruguay speak to a feminist study group in North America on the subject of female spirituality. She reminded them that as women they had three things which a man could never have: breasts, a womb and the existential monthly experience that life comes through the shedding of blood. "The womb is a space of life," she said. "The blood has a language in time, a sense of waiting and of hope in human growth. And breasts are for nurturing. Because of their bodies women can provide a new way of talking about the mystery of God and the ministry of the church."[10]

Therefore it seems that Kierkegaard may not be far wrong in

locating feminine spirituality in devotedness, rather than in the more typical stereotypes of irrationality and intuitiveness. Speaking to this, Nor Hall suggests that "feminine spirituality as appropriated by both male and female is characterized by receptivity, affective response, waiting or attentiveness and the acceptance of pain as intrinsic to the bringing forth of life."[11] Not suprisingly Mary, the mother of Jesus, is often pictured as the ideal contemplative.

The biggest myth to be debunked is that women are spiritually weaker and more prone to sin than men. This is based on the misinterpretation of the term "weaker partner" in 1 Peter 3:7 to mean "weaker in every respect" instead of what was meant as only a physical distinction. This charge has also been made from non-contextual interpretations of 1 Timothy 2:12 where Paul advises that a woman should not teach or have authority over a man, "for Adam was formed first, then Eve. And Adam was not the one deceived; it was the woman who was deceived and became a sinner" (1 Tim 2:13-14).

As I have attempted to show in my book *Married For Good,* Paul *does* argue for a certain priority of the husband in the marital relationship *(priority* but not *rule).* But he does not say that women are typically the first to be deceived. In Ephesus, to which Paul was writing in 1 Timothy, the situation was a replay of the apple in the Garden—the women were the first to be deceived by false teachers and were leading their men astray (2 Tim 3:6). Nowhere, however, does Paul argue that this is always or even normally the case! In this desperate situation Paul forbade the women to teach anybody, even other women or children. And he uses a strong word for "authority over a man," a word which means to "domineer" or to "suppress."

Occasionally a Jewish interpretation of the Old Testament helps break up an evangelical tradition cast in concrete. I heard an Orthodox rabbi justify separating women in the synagogue into a screened area at the back with this stunning argument: "Women are not spiritually inferior, but rather superior. According to Genesis 2 Eve was created after Adam and therefore is closer to the sabbath. Since she was made from man and not from the dust her nature is therefore more spiritually refined and less in need of the synagogue ministry."[12] But the most difficult myth to debunk is the idea that only the male can reflect God.

Male and Female Images of God

One well-kept secret is that *the Bible uses both masculine and feminine images of God.* Genesis 1:27 states God's design: "In the image of God he created him; male and female he created them." Admittedly in the Bible the masculine predominates. This is especially true in the New Testament, because New Testament Christianity was being worked out in an environment of reaction to the mystery religions which preached that the gods had intercourse with one another in heaven.[13]

Nowhere does the Bible encourage us to address God as Mother. But biblical Christians cannot afford to ignore the many Old Testament references to femininity in God. God is a midwife (Ps 22:9), a winged bird under whose wings men take refuge (Ps 36:7). God is both master and mistress (Ps 123:2). The Hebrew word for compassion *(rachmim)* conveys the notion of God's motherly compassion. It is a word that suggests a nurturing womb. In Isaiah 42:13-14 God is seen both as a man of war and as a woman gasping and panting in childbirth.

Commenting on the paucity of feminine images in the New

Testament (except the famous "hen" passage in Matthew 23:37) and the preoccupation of the church with exclusively male images of God, Kenneth Leech notes that it was all too easy for the mother of God (Mariolatry) to replace the missing note of God as a mother. An exalted Mary came to replace the missing biblical dimension of God. Therefore it may be more biblically accurate to speak of God as the Lord whom we have come to know as both Father and Mother, even though we should continue to address God as our Father.[14]

Reasons to Serve Together

Within the priority of the Fatherhood of God it is necessary for us to see both male and female as imaging God. That means that *humanity images God only when there are two complements: male and female,* each being the outer (physical) and the inner (spiritual) complement of the other. The phrase used in Genesis, "helper" (2:18), could better be translated as "helper as his opposite." Each helps the other more completely to resemble and express the nature of God himself. Each person by himself or herself is less than the image of God. The male out of relationship with the female does not express the image of God and therefore can become an idol. The same pertains to the female out of relationship with the male. Couples serving together have a wonderful opportunity to demonstrate the complete image of God.

Jean Vanier, the Canadian who has dedicated himself to establishing communities for the mentally handicapped, comments:

The woman calls forth in man that which is most profound: the heart, tenderness, sensitivity. The man thus becomes more gentle, more attentive, more discerning. He opens himself more to others. The woman awakens his goodness, just as the man awakens all that is most beautiful and feminine in the woman. Man and woman are mirrors to each other; their differences reveal to each other who he or she is.[15]

Beyond such simple statements of complementarity we should not proceed. We are enmeshed in a mystery only partially revealed.

In 1 Corinthians 11:1-10 Paul takes great pains to establish the importance of sexual differences and of maintaining right relationships with the other sex within the Christian community.[16] But in verse 11 Paul seems to turn his own argument on its head when he says that being in Christ is more significant than gender. "In the Lord, however, woman is not independent of man, nor is man independent of woman." *In Christ men are dependent on women!* Then he shows that even in nature there is a reverse dependency: "man is born of woman" (v. 12). He concludes that "everything comes from God."

Because of this biblical emphasis on maintaining differences but developing interdependence, I personally believe Christ would have us move not toward parity in ministry but full partnership. This is true not only for church leadership but also for simple ministries like leading a Bible study group as a couple. Parity communicates sameness and interchangeability; full partnership communicates that the differences can be appreciated and celebrated. When women insist on denying their femininity, as the Corinthian women were by rejecting the veil, then Paul says they have lost the complementarity of life. They are no longer the glory of the image of God. He speaks of the glory that comes to woman when woman is rightly related to man. Had the men been denying their masculinity and their headship, he might have said that the men in Corinth were rejecting their glory by failing to be in right relationship with women. He might well say that to us today.

This is exactly the word we need today for sexual health. On the one hand, we are gloriously different, and these differences are not to be smudged, blurred or diminished in the Christian community. Men should pray, minister and live as men; women should pray, minister and live as women. Paul Tournier addresses this in his latest book, *The Gift of Feeling,* which in the French original was entitled *The Mission of Women.* He believes women have a mission to men, and for God's sake they must not try to be men, nor should men try to be women. C. S. Lewis uses the analogy of the bow and string. Both are needed to make the right sound.

Jean Vanier writes about the impact that this proper alignment can have in our hurting world:

I am convinced that our society desperately needs the reconciliation of men and women in order to build community together. Women, for the most part, exercise authority differently from men, neither better nor worse. At certain times in the history of a community, it might be better to have a man carrying the responsibility; at other times a woman. The essential is that neither exercises authority alone.[17]

In marriage it takes both masculine and feminine spiritualities to be complete in Christ, who is the image of God (Col 1:15). And in ministry it takes both male and female ministers to present an image of God to the world. By serving together, couples in Christ have the opportunity to be gloriously countercultural. Their shared ministry is a profound statement that there is a new creation.

The Synergism of Service

Serving together is like the synergistic effect of two medicines taken together, one enhancing the other. There is a multiple impact. Two are better than one. But two together are also more than the sum of two alone! Ken and Cynthia discovered this, as Cynthia describes their experience of this discipline of shared service.

Ken and I used to teach Sunday school together. We both felt that was an area we were gifted in and were convicted that the students needed both a female as well as a male model as living testimonies of truth. Throughout the years of teaching, we experienced joys and sorrows. Yet we were able to find support from each other. At times we had to sort out conflicts caused by differing paces and expectations from each other. There were eight months in which, having succumbed to manpower pressure, we split up our team to teach different Sunday school classes. The results were disastrous. Thereafter, we vowed never to part in our Sunday school teaching.

Since we moved to a new neighborhood ten months ago, we phased out our responsibilities in our old church. Now we are still exploring areas where we may serve our new home church more effectively. One possible area is couple ministry in home groups formed by the church. Though we have been invited by the pastor to look into doing premarital counseling, we do not want to rush into anything yet. Meanwhile, our shared ministry is in interceding: Sundays we pray for single Christian friends we know; Friday nights, for a number of families; and we pray for our own family on Wednesdays. Interestingly enough, many of our old friends feel we are becoming too inactive in "service." Yet in reality we found ourselves really getting involved in serving God and others through this prayer ministry. The peace and joy of praying regularly for other people is unspeakable.

Putting It into Practice
If you are already involved as partners in ministry, questions 1-4

could help you celebrate and enhance the benefits. If you are wondering what you could do together, try questions 5-9. Answer the questions separately and then share your answers:

If You Are Already Serving Together
1. The area(s) in which I most enjoy serving with my spouse is . . .
2. The spiritual gift or ministry which my spouse contributes to this shared ministry is . . .
3. I experience my spouse's gender spirituality as enriching our ministry in the following way . . .
4. A hazard to our relationship which is posed by our shared service is . . .

If You Would Like to Serve Together
5. Something I can affirm about my spouse's potential for ministry is . . .
6. I think that God normally touches others through my spouse in the following way . . .
7. My spouse's gender spirituality would contribute to a shared ministry in . . .
8. Some of the things I would enjoy doing with my spouse in service to the Lord are (list as many as possible) . . .
9. I suspect that one hazard we would have to overcome in serving together would be . . .

This discussion could lead to an important decision on shared ministry. For further encouragement the short Bible study which follows could open up some new dimension of this spiritual discipline. It concerns a positive New Testament model of team ministry.

Priscilla and Aquila were a remarkable couple. They worked with Paul as tentmaking, self-supporting missionaries. Today we would call them bivocational Christian workers. They served God in three cities: Rome, Corinth and Ephesus. One is never mentioned without the other in Scripture, and Priscilla, the wife, is more often mentioned first than her husband. While we have very little information on them, we may regard them as models of spiritual friendship. Priscilla and Aquila were together a lot. They served, taught and ministered side by side and they put God first.

Read Acts 18:1-4, 18-28; Romans 16:3; 1 Corinthians 16:19 and discuss the following questions:

1. What kinds of pressures and obstacles do you think Priscilla and Aquila might have had to overcome in order to serve together as man and wife?

2. What indications are there that this couple worked as a team (and not merely as a leader with a support partner)?

3. Their sensitive ministry with Apollos is a model of teamwork in ministry. What attitudes could have destroyed their ability to work together with such harmony? What attitudes might have contributed to their full partnership in ministry?

4. What have you learned from Aquila and Priscilla's example that you can apply in your own marriage? In what specific areas can you begin to put this into effect?

5. How do you think your individual sexual spiritualities affect your ability to minister together? How do you understand your spouse better in light of these differences?

6. In what ministry do you think you can best serve God together? What action do you need to take to help make this a reality?

SEXUAL FASTING: THE DISCIPLINE NOBODY WANTS

7

I ASKED MY MARRIAGE CLASS WHAT WOULD BE THE DIS-advantages of accepting the discipline of sexual fasting. With tongue in cheek they quipped, "It causes warts, arthritis, cancer and frustration." But they were right on target with the advantages: "It would allow us to concentrate on prayer or on a specific spiritual issue. But it should be a brief and rare experience." As we talked I suspected that not one of them had ever accepted this discipline voluntarily. Why would they? Who wants to give up sexual privileges?

Why fast when God is pleased when his children delight each other in the marriage bed? We must come to grips with Paul's inspired words in 1 Corinthians 7:5: "Do not deprive each other except by mutual consent and for a time, so that you may devote yourselves to prayer. Then come together again so that Satan will not tempt you because of your lack of self-control." This discipline must be *mutual* ("except by mutual consent"), *brief* ("for a time") and *purposeful* ("that you may devote yourself to prayer"). It is also *dangerous* ("so that Satan will not tempt you because of your lack of self-control").

Mutual Consent: The Biblical Way of Deciding

This is not a discipline to be undertaken when only one partner wants it. It must be approached sensitively, because each spouse wants a responsive and interested sexual partner, not merely a compliant one—and the same goes for abstaining. A friend once said that when he embraced his wife he hoped he would not get mere submission but a living sacrifice! The partner initiating the proposal of sexual fasting needs to make sure that his or her spouse is not merely compliant or wounded by the suggestion.

Not only is sexual fasting the only specific marital discipline outlined in the New Testament, it is the only inspired word given to us on how husbands and wives should make decisions—that is, *mutually*. In Christ the husband does not have decisional sovereignty over his wife. The same deference and sensitivity that must be exercised in the sexual area should carry over to the rest of a couple's life together.

Unfortunately religion often seeks to regulate what God inspires spontaneously. Therefore Pharisaic Judaism found an elaborate way to regulate how long a man and woman should refrain from the sexual embrace as a circumstantial application of Exodus 21:10. In the following quotation from the *Mishnah*, the textbook on Jewish life and thought, it is remarkable that the concern was for the sexual rights and needs of the wife:

If a man vowed to have no intercourse with his wife, the School of Shammai say: [She may consent] for two weeks. And the School of Hillel say: For one week [only]. Disciples [of the Sages] may continue absent for thirty days against the will [of their wives] while they occupy themselves in the study of the Law; and labourers for one week. The *duty of marriage* enjoined in the Law is: every day for them that are unoccupied; twice a week for labourers; once a week for ass-drivers; once every thirty days for camel-drivers; and once every six months for sailors.

This quotation definitely favors the unemployed man—who is obligated to perform his marital duty to his wife *every day!* The *Mishnah* continues with another quotation dealing with the penalties against a woman who refuses her marital duty.

If a woman will not consent to her husband he may reduce her *Ketubah* [the sum of money pledged by the bridegroom to the bride in the case of his death or divorce] by seven *denars* [2 denars = 1 shekel—the price of a lamb was about 2 shekels] for every week. Rabbi Judah says: Seven *tropaics* [4 tropaics = 1 shekel]. For how long may he reduce it? [For a time] corresponding to the sum of her *Ketubah*. Rabbi Jose says: He may go on reducing it continually, that if perchance an inheritance falls to her from elsewhere he may claim it from her. So, too, if a husband will not consent to his wife, her *Ketubah* may be increased by three *denars* a week. Rabbi Judah says: Three *tropaics*.[1]

How much simpler, indeed sublime, are Paul's inspired words in 1 Corinthians 7:5. Sexual fasting must be *mutually* desired; both husband and wife must agree to the fast.

For a Time: A Discipline for Rare Moments

Gordon Fee's masterful commentary on 1 Corinthians shows convincingly that the context of 1 Corinthians 7:5 is not the situation where the Corinthian Christians were needing to be exhorted to shut down their sexual activity in marriage in order to spend more time in prayer. It was just the reverse.[2] There was a strong element in the Corinthian church that looked down on sexual intercourse as something less worthy, belonging to this earthly existence which has substantially passed away now that the Spirit has come. There seems to be some evidence for the presence of "eschatological women" who thought of themselves as already having obtained the resurrection of the dead, who were like the angels in heaven, neither giving nor being given in marriage (Lk 20:35). These superspiritual Christians were above something as lowly as marital intercourse.

This is remarkably similar to the view presently used to justify the superior life of the virgin and celibate priest in the Roman Catholic Church. Pope John Paul II writes that

> in virginity or celibacy, the human being is awaiting, also in a bodily way, the eschatological marriage of Christ with the Church. . . . The celibate person thus anticipates in his or her flesh the new world of the future resurrection. . . . Virginity or celibacy, by liberating the human heart in a unique way, "so as to make it burn with greater love for God and all humanity," bears witness that the Kingdom of God and His justice is that pearl of great price which is preferred to every other value. . . . It is for this reason that the Church, throughout her history, has always defended the superiority of this charism to that of mar-

riage by reason of the wholly singular link which it has with the Kingdom of God.[3]

Paul's word to the superspiritual Christians in Corinth is "Stop depriving each other!" (7:5). Because the sexual act is good, unitive (6:16) and holy, and because neither person has the authority over his or her own body, sexual intercourse is not one's marital right but the marital right of one's partner. It is not a right to be taken, but given. As Gordon Fee says, "Paul puts sexual relations within Christian marriage on much higher ground than one finds in most cultures, including the church, where sex is often viewed as the husband's privilege and the wife's obligation."[4] Correcting superspirituality is the occasion for mentioning the discipline of sexual fasting: "Do not defraud or deprive each other except . . ." This is not a command or a law, but an exception, a rare discipline for rare occasions.

The discipline of sexual fasting should spring from a high view of sex, not from a low view. It is remarkable to me that a celibate Roman Catholic, Jean Vanier, has written some of the deepest words on the sacramental nature of the sex act. They are worthy of inclusion here:

The relationship between [husband and wife] is so precious, not only for the two of them but also for the children, for society, for God, that the Father himself has promised always to come and help them as they journey towards a more profound unity. This union between man and woman is sacred. It is in the image of God, the Father, Son and Spirit. It is, above all, the first human union, the source of all other human unions.

This is why the union of man and woman is a sacrament. It is announced before the Church and confirmed by the Church. It is a sacred sign, instituted by Jesus. It is a place of encounter with God; he is present in this union and always comes to the aid of the spouses. He helps them to profit from all the difficult elements in marriage. . . .

The foundations of this union are in the desire of the Father that man and woman, despite their wounds and their psychological and human poverty, should share in his trinitarian life and in his merciful love. . . . The union becomes eucharistic, an act of thanksgiving for having refound unity.

This is why the genital organs are sacred. They are reserved for a divine work: to be at the same time a sign of trinitarian life and a source of life. These organs must be used only to live a life of love and a covenant which has been blessed and confirmed by God himself. Their usage outside this covenant traps the man and the woman each in his or her own isolation. The sexual act, instead of being a source and sign of hope, becomes a cause of despair. It awakens that which is most intimate, most sacred, most vulnerable in the human heart without being able to fulfill it, or to respond to the deep need to be loved with a total love. Only when it is enveloped in the presence of Jesus can the love of husband and wife deepen and bring them profound peace. Their hearts are thirsting, not for a passing love, not for a subjective pleasure, but for a total and eternal love which will bring them out of their isolation into unity.[5]

It is just like our God not to tell us how often we may have sex in marriage, but rather to tell us how seldom we should refrain. Like the fruits of the Spirit, you can express your love to each other all you wish: "Against such . . . there is no law" (Gal 5:23). In one sense you can never get or give too much—as long as it is love that is shared and not lust. So this discipline must be brief, "for a time."

Devoting Yourself to Prayer: Purposeful Fasting

Perhaps this discipline is exactly what some people expect in a book on marriage spirituality. In one of the very few books that deals with spiritual formation in marriage, Evelyn and James Whitehead concede that even to talk of spiritual disciplines suggests "a split between the worlds of spirit and flesh—the spirit which is suspiciously invisible and otherworldly, and the flesh which is too visible and most unruly. When this split is in force, spirituality most often has to do with abstaining from making love, rather than becoming good at it."[6] In point of fact we might accept the discipline of sexual fasting for exactly the same reasons we might accept the discipline of food fasting—to temporarily renounce some activity that is good in itself for the greater good of being intensively focused on God himself.

Paul said that the reason to refrain from the normal "ritual" of the marriage covenant is *solely* for "prayer and fasting." It is *not* for getting back at one's spouse for an offense, not for a higher spirituality, not for more time for Christian service. This discipline should be undertaken only if it helps a couple to seek God together in a *focused* way.

I want to express this carefully because this book is about marriage spirituality in the context of the total marriage experience, *including* the sexual embrace. God receives *all* the experiences of our marriages, all of its earthiness, all of its hurts and hopes. Sex is sacred to couples in love with God. But sometimes even good gifts should be put aside to possess a greater good.

Few writers have developed a model of contemplative marriage spirituality which reconciles the mutual attachment and sexual bond of a couple with their desire to be attentive to God.[7] But the apostle Paul himself gives us the clue to this in a very difficult passage in 1 Corinthians 7, where he discusses the advisability of remaining single for God. He says, "Let those who have wives live as though they had none" (v. 29 RSV). The reason behind this hard word is that Paul wants believers to be single-minded toward God, whether married or single.

Paul's solution to being undividedly devoted to the Lord whether married or single is to view one's life as an opportunity to serve Christ and his kingdom—versus seeing life as merely a means to personal fulfillment. We can be married *for God* or single *for God,* not merely married or single. To the *unmarried*—whether the single, once married or would-be married—Paul would say, "Do not dream. Marriage is not the kingdom of God. You may live a complete Christian life as a single person by living completely for God." To the *unhappily married* Paul would say, "Do not despair. There is more to the Christian life than your marriage. Be married for God!" To the *happily married,* Paul would say the most disturbing word: "Do not presume the blessing of a happy marriage is identical with the blessing of Christ who said: 'Blessed are the poor in spirit . . . [and] the pure in heart, for they will see God' " (Mt 5:3-12). It is a contemplative marriage that seeks God first of all.

The difference between meditation and contemplation may serve to bring this point home. *Meditation* can be defined as the process of moving from the things of this world to the things of God. Married people are called to have the kind of meditative marriage where this kind of focus can happen. But there is more to the spiritual life than meditation, just as there is more to marriage spirituality than bustling Christian activity.

For instance, I have heard it advised that you should not marry unless you can serve God better with your spouse than you could as a single person. But that brings a utilitarian standard into marriage. Marriage is then useful to get more work done for God on earth. But what if your husband gets ill, or one of you cannot take the pressures of certain kinds of service, or you come home from overseas service ill, or one of you has an emotional breakdown? Then service for God as a motive for marriage becomes obsolete.

The mystery of marriage goes much deeper than some efficiencies of production in Christian ministry. As we have seen, there is something within the marriage relationship itself, independent of its fruits, that is a revelation of God himself. Also, this covenant relationship is itself a sacramental means of coming to God.

Having undivided devotion to the Lord requires centering not on the things of God but on God himself. And so a *contemplative marriage* begins to make more sense. Contemplation can be defined as the process of moving from attending to the *things of God*—service, activities, doctrine—to being preoccupied *with God himself.* One may be contemplative while enjoying the sexual embrace, but there will be times—perhaps in the middle of making a major decision—when focusing on God together will require sexual fasting. In this case contemplation may involve turning from the good gift of marital sexuality to attend to God himself, the greatest good of all. But the discipline is dangerous.

Avoiding Satan's Temptation: The Danger of Abstinence

Paul's advice to abstain "for a time . . . so that Satan will not tempt you because of your lack of self-control" rings true. A long period of sexual abstinence is abnormal. Paul does not recommend this discipline because there is anything unholy or unspiritual about the sexual embrace (although many Christians firmly believe this). Before I married, an older Christian once remarked to me that men who really love God do not make love often with their wives. Paul would disagree—and so do I. The "spiritual" thing is to express love and meet needs, not to give your partner reason to be tempted to a sexual affair with someone else who is more attentive.

On a humorous note let me tell you about Greg and Cynthia. They came to a "spiritual friendship weekend" at our local monastery all set to try everything at once (even though we had not advised this). In addition to a discipline of silence which they committed to keep for two days (hardly a good thing to do on a couple retreat), they wanted to try fasting from food. As though this were not enough they took on the unpopular discipline of sexual fasting. I must stress that this was not what we taught but what they came intending to do. What made the sexual fasting so difficult, perhaps even unwise, is that Greg and Cynthia came to the retreat after a long period of heavy stressful work and ministry. Their sexual love had been infrequent, perfunctory and relegated to the last weary moments of the day. They had been giving each other leftovers. At the conference they settled into a beautiful room overlooking the Fraser Valley and a double bed. Now they had the leisure to enjoy each other as well as to pray. But then there was the discipline. As the evening wore on, Greg could not keep his silence so he started sending notes to Cynthia. The next morning they shared their notes with me, and I laughed uproariously at the record of their joyless devotions.

Greg first wrote, "I think we have the nicest room. I don't think we deserve it." Cynthia resisted answering. Then Greg suggested, "Let's go for a walk before it rains, before darkness hits, or some other calamity."

Once again Cynthia kept her discipline of silence. Greg then wrote these words, "I'm sure this place will run out of hot water soon. I think I'll have a shower before there is only cold water left."

Hours passed and Greg's physical appetites were making themselves known. "I'm hungry," he wrote next. "Do you think we could sneak down to the kitchen and steal some bread even though supper is over?" Cynthia did not bite. Greg was determined not to miss the three-course cooked breakfast the next day. (As an ultimate irony Greg, of all the conferees, slept in, missed breakfast, roared down in the morning only to find one bowl left of sugar-coated Fruit Loops, an insult to his health-food sensitivities!) But the final entry in their notebook must have been made about 10:00 P.M. Greg wrote, "Give me a hug." Cynthia wrote, "I knew you wouldn't last!" She bit. But there would be another time, a better time to practice the discipline nobody wants. This couple found themselves a little later facing a great decision. They came to their fasting with a heart full of love for each other. And accepting a short period of sexual restraint by mutual agreement did bring focus to their prayers. And God marvelously met them.

Putting It into Practice

Talk together about what you have learned from this chapter about the place of sexual affection in your marriage.

Recall a situation in the past when the acceptance of this discipline would have helped you gain focus in your prayers together.

What situations in the present or possible situations in the future might be good occasions to practice this discipline?

How would you like your spouse to present the idea to you when he or she thinks the time is right?

Share together how occasions of involuntary sexual fasting—for example, for sickness—could have taken a deeper meaning if both partners took this opportunity for a deeper prayer life and to express love for one another through other languages?

OBEDIENCE: DOING GOD'S WILL TOGETHER

8

GAIL AND I HAD A BIG DECISION BEFORE US. SHOULD WE leave the church where I was serving in order to take up a tent-making carpentry job and begin a new mission? Or did God have something else for us? With only days left to make a decision, God surprisingly offered me everything I had ever wanted vocationally.[1] I had three ministry goals for my lifetime: first, to be pastor of the church where I was currently serving; second, to be chaplain of a particular Canadian university; and third, to teach in a lay training center. In our crucial decision-making week I received a letter from the president of the univrsity inviting me to apply for the chaplain's post and a phone call about teaching in the training center. Both were opportunities for *me*—but were they God's will for *us* as a couple?

If two of you on earth agree about anything you ask . . . (Mt 18:19).

We were considering a radical alternative—doing so-called secular work while planting multiple house churches in the inner city. This had not been one of my three original goals. Godly advisers thought that we had lost our marbles and warned us that we were committing vocational suicide. We would be "wasting" ourselves, they said, in carpentry and a tiny church. As our children were still preteens, we decided that such a controversial, difficult path had to be decided by the parents alone, especially as things might go wrong. We would have to take the risks for them and trust them to God. Young children cannot handle the responsibility of complicated or painful family decisions. (Later we made another vocational decision *as a family* because our teenage children would be more affected by a move to another city than Gail and I would. They were old enough to help us discern God's will for the family.)

We had wrung an important spiritual principle out of two decades of spiritual friendship: *if it is not God's will for both of us, it is probably not God's will, no matter how much one spouse believes he or she has God's guidance.* So I wrote the president, made a declining phone call and donned my nail belt to do God's will *for us,* not merely for me.

Christ leads married people as *couples,* not merely as individual husbands and wives. The discipline of obedience is a spiritual process for a couple. It clears a path to God which is wide enough for two, as do the other disciplines in this book. In reality this turns out to be a complicated process, as Gail and I have discovered. Indeed, we have found that there are several myths about guidance that need to be debunked by couples who want to do God's will together.

Guidance Myths for Couples

Myth number one: God has a wonderful plan for your life together. A plan is like a blueprint of a construction project which must be followed in every detail. If you fail to obey one detail, you may have to start over again. People who view guidance as finding that "wonderful plan," self-consciously take the pulse of their spiritual lives to see if they are in the center of God's will. One false move and it is back to *Go* to start the game over again! But sometimes you cannot start again. This myth is especially dangerous when one has come to the sad conclusion that he or she somehow missed God's plan for marriage. But for me another area of learning brought this home.

The only thing I can remember being said by a preacher on the weekend I was converted was a lie. The preacher said, "God called me into the mission field. I hesitated to go; so God fixed it so I could never go. He made me have a motorcycle accident, and now I have a lame leg and every mission board rejects me!" Fortunately I was apprehended by Christ and not by that preacher. But I have often reflected that one would be more likely to hate rather than love a master who never gave a second chance. Imagine being doomed to a second-class Christian life because you made one wrong move! Our God has something better than a plan; he has a *purpose.*

The difference between following a plan and a purpose is like the difference between following a road map and canoeing downstream in a fast-flowing river. The road map leaves little room for change and none for error. In a stream there is plenty of room to maneuver provided one is going with the water and abandoned to the flow. God's purpose is that we will know him and share in the coming of his kingdom. There are many different ways of doing this. Because of a mistake—real or presumed—we are not doomed to missing God's will for our lives.

Myth number two: God's will is hard to discover. Pagans think this way. They make much of guidance by divination and signs. But for couples in Christ the will of God is transparently clear in Scripture. God's grand plan is to renew everything in Christ (Eph 1:22-23; 3:10-11; Rev 21:5). This is far more important than knowing which car to buy or whether to stay at home for a vacation. It has been said that life is like a card game with three parts: the rules we play by, the hand that is dealt to us and the way we play that hand.

The Bible calls the rules by which we play and the hand we were dealt *the will of God.* Then the Bible tells us to apply wisdom and to let the Spirit guide us as we play out the hand given to us (Ps 48:14; 25:9; Prov 3:5-6; Jn 16:13). Ninety-nine out of a hundred choices couples make are decided by applying sound judgment and prayer to the will of God they already know in Scripture. To speak of seeking guidance from God directly may be more pagan than Christian. Couples in Christ have something better than guidance; they have a Guide.

Myth number three: God wants to make the decisions for you. He doesn't—in spite of fervent requests to the contrary. Many couples pray fervently for God to control them and then wonder why he does not answer that prayer. Our God respects his God-imaging creatures too much to depersonalize us. Christ, the head, wants his body to become mature, not stay immature; and so he refuses to make decisions for us or to program our lives to look like so many assembly-line robots (Eph 4:13, 15). Jesus said to his disciples, "I no longer call you servants. . . . I have called you friends, for everything that I learned from my Father I have made known to you" (Jn 15:15).

Gail and I would have felt relieved of responsibility if God had made our decision for us, but that would also have relieved us of the dignity of being friends of Jesus. God's goal for our marriages, as micro-churches, is for growth in Christ, the Head (Eph 4:15), and that cannot happen if spouses or couples passively wait until decisions are made for them by their spouses or by God!

Myth number four: God's leading is often discerned by supernatural signs and messages. God confirmed our decision to start Dayspring Fellowship, our inner-city church, with an encouraging prophecy. We *did* have many signs that God was with us, especially when we desperately needed encouragement. But none of these signs by itself was a basis for decision. God's will had to be the right thing for the totality of our lives, including our children.

It is dangerous to make major life decisions on the basis of a prophecy, an immediate word from God given by a fellow believer. A prophecy should confirm what we know to be God's will in other ways (1 Cor 14:3). In the Acts of the Apostles, believers were constantly using their redeemed judgment (Acts 6:3; 15:36; 20:16; also Rom 1:10-13; 1 Cor 16:4-9; 2 Cor 1:5—2:4). *All* cases of supernatural signs, like the vision of the unclean animals given to Peter (Acts 10:9-23), were unsought. Couples sometimes wait for a mystical revelation when they should be practicing what they already know to be God's will.

Myth number five: God's will is normally associated with "open doors." What do you do when you are confronted, as Gail and I were, with three open doors—all personal dreams—and one door slightly ajar, with problems on the other side? Some open doors of opportunity (1 Cor 16:9) must be entered, but some closed doors must be battered down for the sake of God's purpose (Acts 4:18-20). Being guided by open and closed doors means *being conformed to* circumstances rather than *transforming* circumstances by doing the will of God.

We are called to walk by faith, not by sight. Walking by faith means understanding our lives by faith in God, not by the circumstances we find ourselves in. Usually when we talk about other people's lives, we are very selective in what we say was the will of God—such as when something goes well and their Christian life seems fruitful. Did Carey do the will of God when he ministered in India for fourteen years before there was a conversion? Sometimes the "signs" will seem negative, but we must still go on, trusting God with the results. Walking by faith means seeking our contentment, peace, security or our joy in God, rather than focusing on how well things are going.

If we walk by faith, we will not always be able to give a reason for what we feel or do. That is the nature of faith. Our reasons will always leave someone unsatisfied. Walking by faith means that we cannot say when someone *else* did the will of God. We must only answer to God for ourselves. Reluctantly, Paul's friends said "The Lord's will be done," when Paul took the Gentile gift to Jerusalem against his friends' prophetic warning (Acts 21:4-14). But Paul must have thought, "That, my friends, is exactly what I am doing . . . God's will!" Paul had had a word from God to build bridges between the Gentile and Jewish believers (Gal 1:16; 2:9; Rom

15:15-29), and no closed doors would stop him. The same should be true for couples doing God's will.

Myth number six: When you make a mistake, you have to go back and start again, if you can. Gail and I had ample opportunity to think we made a mistake. The work was very difficult. We ran into relationship problems in the leadership. I had to work harder in carpentry than I had anticipated to support my family, which added weekend jobs to my workweek.

In marriage this myth is especially dangerous. When things get tough, some couples assume they married out of the will of God, get a divorce and start again. But the fact that things go wrong and life becomes hard is no indication that we are out of the will of God. God might be pruning and disciplining us because he loves us. When Paul was in his worst predicaments—stoned, dragged out of town, slandered—we know by hindsight that he was definitely in the will of God. There is a heretical notion today that the will of God will lead to an easy, prosperous and trouble-free existence. Paul was just as much in the will of God in prison as he was on Mars Hill. He apparently never regretted taking the love gift from the Gentiles to the poor saints in Jerusalem, even though it meant shuffling from prison to prison for the rest of his life.

Grace means the exact opposite of redoing our lives. It enables us to live fully in the present, free from permanent harm from our pasts, anticipating a glorious future. God in his sovereignty incorporates both our mistakes and the mistakes of others that impinge on our lives into his grand purpose for us. Joseph said to his brothers who sold him into slavery in Egypt, "You intended to harm me, but God intended it for good" (Gen 50:20). With such a God one can never lose! The only big mistake is not to *want* to do God's will.

Wanting Unity

When Paul told the Ephesians to "find out what pleases the Lord" (5:10), he addressed the heart of being guided. As we shall see, God is more easily pleased than most parents—and some spouses! There are at least three ways to please God as we seek his will as a couple. The whole letter of Paul to the Ephesians is a statement of God's determined purpose to make unity out of diversity. The crowning example of this is the incorporation of *both* Jews and Gentiles into a whole new humanity (2:15-16), making them fellow citizens. Neither Jew nor Gentile would be second-class in Christ.

When I was teaching Ephesians in the Divinity School of the African Brotherhood Church in Kenya I got a glimpse of how radical this double reconciliation really is—God with humanity and humanity with humanity. I had drawn a broken wall on the blackboard of this simple classroom, reflecting as I did on how lost I feel without an overhead projector. "Last week we learned that the work of Christ is like destroying the wall that separated Jews and Gentiles in the Jerusalem Temple [Eph 2:14]. That wall symbolized the hostility between them. But tell me now, for what groups of people would it take a miracle to bring them together in one family in your country? Are there tribes which one hardly ever finds together, even in church?"

There was an embarrassing silence. Then Ezekiel (that is his baptism name) put up his hand. "Walimu," he said, "the Kamba and Masai tribes are the greatest enemies." I found out, however, that there are churches in which these irreconcilably separated peoples *are* together. Our class explored the exciting reality of the church as a super-tribe that encompassed all tribes.

In chapter four of Ephesians, Paul applies this doctrine of unity to the church; in chapter five, to marriage; in chapter six, to parents and children, to slaves and masters—even to employers and employees. Mutual submission, in humility and gentleness, that acknowledges the difference between peoples is the relational sign that a community is being filled with the Holy Spirit (4:3; 5:18, 21).

Sometimes I wonder if God is interested in anything but unity. *For husbands and wives to talk, pray, listen and wait until they have a common mind is not only a good marital strategy. It is the only biblical way for couples to make decisions.* God is apparently more interested in husband-wife unity than he is interested in getting his job done. I repeat that if it is not God's will for both, it is probably not God's will, no matter how much one spouse believes he or she has God's guidance.

Wanting the Guide More than Guidance

Surprisingly, the Bible has no word for guidance. Instead, the Bible gives us three images of the Guide and the guided. There is the *sheep and Shepherd* (Ps 23; Jn 10). The Shepherd "calls" (Jn 10:3), "leads" (10:3) and the sheep "listen to his voice" (10:3), "know his voice" (10:4) and "follow him" (10:4).

There is the parental image of *father-mother* and *son-daughter*. God the Father sends the spirit of his Son into our hearts giving us the freedom, motivation and privileges of being in his family (Gal 4:1-7; Rom 8:15-17). Just as parents move from closely supervising their children with detailed instructions to giving them freedom and responsibility, God—who is more than the words *father* or *mother* can communicate—is determined to make us mature in Christ (Col 1:28; Eph 4:13).

Finally, there is the image of *friend with friend* (Jn 15:13-16).

Our friend Jesus tells us his father's business and purpose so we will know the Father's mind. Unlike slaves, we are called to make decisions in such a way that we do what he wants and commands. All three images communicate that the relationship with the Guide is more important than getting the exact details of the Guide's instructions. The great benefit of the discipline of couple obedience is not that a couple learns how to make good decisions, but that a couple gets to know God better. Couple obedience, like all other marital disciplines, is a pathway to God.

Trusting God When You Have Made a Decision
Have you ever been plagued by second thoughts—even about things you cannot change? "What if I married that other girl, took that other job or joined that other church?" *When you have made a decision, there is no need to keep looking back.* We are not supposed to look back after we have put our hands to the plowshare of the kingdom (Lk 9:62). But many Christians settle with installing a rearview mirror on their plowshares! The effect is the same. They are immobilized.

I like the way Persian rugs are made. Two long poles are erected on which the body of the rug is stretched. On one side is the master rug-maker who, knowing the overall intended design, calls out the color and position of the threads for the weavers standing on the opposite side to insert. Inevitably there are errors in communication and understanding. The designer, seeing an obvious error from his side that is not apparent to the weavers, makes allowances by redesigning the overall plan. His purpose is more important than his detailed plan. Our God can make something beautiful out of our lives no matter what we have done. Otherwise the gospel is good news only for the flawless.

Gail and I have often been tempted to consider whether we made the right decision during that significant week in 1975, but we know that the only mistake we could have made would have been not to *want* to do God's will. Sometimes we do not find out exactly *how* we did the will of the Lord until long after. Now with several years of inspired hindsight, we know that we did God's will that week. We also know that our principle of guidance has never proved untrue, and so bears repeating here: *If it is not God's will for both of us, it is probably not God's will, no matter how much one spouse believes he or she has God's guidance.*

Marriage is a profound opportunity to discover the truth of Jesus' words: "If two of you on earth agree about anything you ask for, it will be done for you by my Father in heaven." Jesus gives the reason for such unity and power in decision making in the next verse. "For where two or three come together in my name, there am I with them" (Mt 18:19-20). This makes the discipline of obedience part of a couple's path to God.

Putting It into Practice
Take this chapter as an opportunity to work on one area of decision-making in your marriage or in the life of one spouse. Perhaps it is a vocational decision or a decision to move or a need to redirect energies toward the family. If one does not feel ready to do this right now, it would be better to come back to this exercise at a later time in which you both agree to participate fully. However, one partner should not postpone decision-making indefinitely thus holding the other "hostage" by refusing to participate at all. It is possible to use lack of interest as a way of controlling the decision-making process. Select a matter which you would like to resolve in such a way that you can eventually say, "We did God's will

together." When you have agreed on this prayerfully, ask God to help you work through the following steps:

1. Are we being hindered in doing God's will by any of the "guidance" myths?

God has a blueprint plan for our life.

God's will is hard to discover.

God wants to make the decision for us.

We expect God to show us by a supernatural sign or message.

God's will is associated with "open doors."

If we make a mistake, we must start over again.

2. Are we willing to wait until we agree together before either of us acts on this? If not, why not?

What benefits will be obtained in this matter if we wait until we can agree together?

What difficulties might we experience if one of us goes ahead, believing it is "the Lord's will"?[2]

3. In what ways might we want guidance more than we want the Guide?

4. Recall some specifics of how you as a couple have experienced the Lord as shepherd, parent and friend?

5. If you have not yet started praying together as a couple, this would be a good time to start! Most couples find that they need to come back to the Lord again and again on matters like these until their hearts are agreed on the will of God. Claim the promise for yourself: "If two of you on earth agree about anything you ask for, it will be done for you by my Father in heaven."

CONFESSION: THE SURGERY OF FORGIVENESS

9

D O YOU THINK I SHOULD TELL MY HUSBAND THAT I HAVE had an affair?" When I am asked this question from time to time in the context of pastoral ministry I am aware that this is a profound issue of marriage spirituality. I dare not give advice. But I am obligated by Christian love to explore the alternatives, the "saving lie" on the one hand—a story that will maintain the shaky stability of the marriage—or confession on the other hand. But I know that confession will probably have devastating results. Some marriages do not survive the surgery of confession in such radical situations.. Perhaps they would not have survived the "saving lie" either.

Usually it is helpful to make a full confession to a trusted Christian leader first, to get rid of the garbage. It is crucial for the sinning partner to seek the Lord's forgiveness first. Often we do not feel forgiven until we hear Christ's word on human lips. Usually a person so burdened with the weight of a broken relationship needs help to find the right time and right way to make such a confession to the offended spouse. But I know that whoever confesses such a sin and begs for forgiveness will never be the same again. Nor will the marriage.

The Inner Logic of Confession

Personally, I find it inconceivable that two disciples of Jesus—in this case, joined in marriage—can "walk in the light" and have fellowship unless there is full confession and forgiveness. Confession for the Christian is not merely a spiritual discipline, but a grace: "If we walk in the light, as he is in the light, we have fellowship with one another, and the blood of Jesus, his Son, purifies us from all sin" (1 Jn 1:7). Because marriage is the most intimate of human relationships, there are daily opportunities to wound and therefore daily opportunities to practice the discipline of confession.

The spiritual counterpart to confession is forgiveness: first for the offender by the offended. But forgiveness is not complete until the sinner forgives him or herself, a sign of practical belief that Jesus did enough on the cross to atone for the sin, and no more crucifixion is needed. Sometimes, where forgiveness is not given by the offended, the offender must rest in God's forgiveness for him or herself. This can be a spiritual struggle. It always takes time—

sometimes a long time.

In Ephesians 6 the apostle Paul says that "our struggle is *not* against flesh and blood" (v. 12, emphasis mine). Elsewhere Paul deals with conflict in our spiritual life under the category of "flesh," what human nature has become through sin (Rom 7—8). That battle goes on *within* the Christian. But we misunderstand spiritual warfare, as Jerome and Thomas Aquinas did, if we think it is merely war against passions. We are fighting a whole system, indeed a system of systems that Paul calls "rulers . . . authorities . . . the powers of this dark world" and "the spiritual forces of evil in the heavenly realms" (Eph 6:12). The spreading plague of divorce and widespread sexual unfaithfulness, not to mention "simple" selfishness, are merely tips of an evil iceberg. The idolatrous demands made by some employers or professional societies and the narcissistic drive toward personal self-fulfillment are covenant-threatening forces from the "other side."

No couple in Christ can afford to ignore the reality of a formidable enemy to their marriage. The devil is a sinister spiritual being with personal characteristics who has colonized the structures of life, including marriage, to wean us from dependence on God. Satan is the archenemy of marriage spirituality because he knows the awesome power of unity in Christ. Since he is a master of deception, he will come to us not so much in the obviously Satanic, but in seemingly spiritual ways—such as in condemning a fellow sinner. He is called "the accuser of our brothers" (Rev 12:10), and marriage partners may unwittingly be his accomplices by joining Satan in condemning a child of God—one's own spouse or even oneself.

The most common entrée for the devil in a Christian marriage is simply the refusal to forgive. Paul warns us, "Do not let the sun go down while you are still angry, and do not give the devil a foothold" (Eph 4:26-27). Failure to confess and failure to forgive both lead to doubting the goodness of God (and one's spouse) and, finally, to a bitter spirit. Satan is determined to split up Christian marriages. The widespread breakup of the marriages of Christian leaders in North America is part of a sinister plot from the dark side of the universe which we have unconsciously aided and abetted. May it be said of us that "we are not unaware of his schemes" (2 Cor 2:11). The discipline of confession is crucial to winning this spiritual battle.

Confessing Our Faults

We need to exercise the discipline of confession for both words and deeds, and for offenses ranging from adultery to domestic financial mismanagement. But we also need to confess our faults, our weaknesses, our predispositions to err.

I have a tendency to overwork. Whether I have a drivenness to seek the approval of others or am a person experiencing the profoundly liberating effect of being called by God (I suspect it is some of both), I want to give one hundred-and-twenty-five per cent. Sometimes I feel a little like Steven Spielberg who complains that he sometimes has so many ideas for films when he wakes up that he can hardly eat his breakfast. I love what I do . . . sometimes too much. While I believe that marriage and family are a higher priority than ministry and work, I sometimes sacrificed Gail, my parents (when they were alive) and my children. This needs to be confessed. And I need not only Gail's forgiveness but her help.

James 5:16 says, "Confess your faults one to another, and pray one for another, that ye may be healed" (KJV). This means confessing our weak spots, like acknowledging fault lines in the structure of the earth. It allows our spouses to pray about our potential to sin and to practice preventive healing. Faults are where earthquakes are likely to wreak their greatest damage. Our marital fault lines are where stresses can bring tragedy. But the grace of our Lord is that strength comes through weakness (2 Cor 12:9-10). If we are honest with each other about our faults, and turn to Christ at this very point of human need, our weaknesses can turn out to be assets in building spiritual friendship.

What makes Christianity unique is that God shines through us not *in spite of* our weaknesses, but *because* of them. Paul said that we can take the veil off our faces now that we are in Christ, thus revealing what is really going on inside (2 Cor 3:18). We can fearlessly confess our true state to each other because we are "being changed into his likeness from one degree of glory to another" (3:18 RSV).

There is a transfiguration going on. But we cannot see what God is doing if we cover up our sins and our faults or refuse to take them seriously when they are confessed.

Confession is to marriage what baptism is to the Christian life. More than rituals, they are tools of transformation. Peter says baptism is "an appeal to God for a clear conscience, through the resurrection of Jesus Christ" (1 Pet 3:21 RSV). Baptism is a stake driven in, an acted prayer, a cry for cleansing, a nonrefundable investment of faith. Confession is the same. It is an appeal for a clear conscience in the marriage and has the same nonrefundable impact. When confession is met with forgiveness—in the case of actual sin—Satan is defeated, our spiritual enemies are sent scurrying for cover, strongholds are demolished by divine power and God gives relational peace (2 Cor 10:4).

Why then are we so reluctant to practice this discipline?

Because we have not allowed ourselves to be broken. Our terrible pride forces us to erect walls of self-defense or facades of wholeness when in reality we are broken bread and crushed grapes waiting to be made into bread and wine. Like the Pharisee praying in the Temple, we would rather justify ourselves than justify God (Lk 18:9-14). Ironically, the tax collector who justified God and abased himself went home justified and exalted, while the self-justifying Pharisee went home unjustified. It is the gospel principle: "Everyone who exalts himself will be humbled, and he who humbles himself will be exalted" (v. 14).

Marriage is exactly the environment in which the gospel can become a day-to-day reality. Spirituality is incurably domestic. So is the gospel. If we justify God—in affirming his view of the situation and wanting him to be honored—we will not be justifying ourselves. But the miracle of the gospel is that God, because of his work on the cross, is able to justify the ungodly! From a human perspective, the gospel is scandalously immoral—and every Pharisee has seen it this way (Lk 15:25-32). But faith seizes it as a wonderful gift and revels in it.

By confession, we have everything to gain and nothing to lose but our self-righteousness. This kind of brokenness can make our marriages whole, especially if it is met with forgiveness.

Giving Covenant Forgiveness

Forgiveness involves remembering, forgetting, canceling, prizing and creating. In order to forgive, we need to *remember* that we ourselves are forgiven completely and fully by God. Our debts toward one another are miniscule by comparison. We need to remember our vows and promises. When we pledged our troth to each other, we said that only death would separate us. Adultery is grounds for forgiveness, not divorce. Lesser sins are likewise for-giveable.

Forgiveness means *forgetting*. Perhaps the fact that something has happened, especially something as violent as adultery or phys-ical abuse, may make it near impossible for it to be forgotten. It is surely one of the mysteries of God's greatness that God himself does forget our sins. He says, "I will forgive their wickedness and will remember their sins no more" (Jer 31:34; see also Heb 8:12). We can at least learn this from our ultimate High Priest: forgive-ness precedes forgetting. The more we forgive, the more we forget. Perhaps forgetting is not the inability to call up a recorded fact from the deep memory of our minds. Rather it is the willful deci-sion not to keep calling it up for the purposes of reminder, as a weapon, or as an instrument to put another down. Now that is creative forgetting and it is exactly what forgiveness inspires. By faith we can regard it, even in remembrance, as an opportunity to affirm the sufficiency of Jesus. The scars of Jesus on his hands and feet were, after the resurrection, not merely marks of human vio-lence but tangible signs for Thomas and other seeking doubters to believe. This is constructive remembering, using each remem-brance as an opportunity to affirm the grace of God.

Canceling the debt is something that God has done with our sins. He does not offer us an easy repayment schedule, reduced interest or tradeoffs. He does not ask us to give him a lifetime of service in exchange for full forgiveness. That would be conditional forgiveness, contractual forgiveness, not new covenant forgive-ness. Similarly we need to cancel our spouse's debt. This means no repayment, no regular reminders, no tradeoffs. The past is in the past. We must free our spouses to be as though the sin had not taken place.

138 _____ MARRIAGE SPIRITUALITY

Prizing the relationship is what we do both by confession and by forgiveness. Through telling the whole truth we risk rejection. But we also affirm that having a genuine relationship is more important to us than maintaining the shell of a formal connection. Confession is a relational compliment. So is forgiveness. By forgiving our spouse, even before there is repentance, we are stating that the relationship is more important than the behavior. Often forgiveness inspires repentance, inspires confession.

There is a risk in forgiving even before there is repentance, the risk that it seems not to matter. This can degenerate into what Dietrich Bonhoeffer called "cheap grace," grace that lets someone continue in sin without changing his or her lifestyle. Cheap grace appears merely to condone sin. It lets sinners off scot-free before they know they are offenders. Costly grace, in contrast, lets the sinner experience the weight of his or her deed. Sometimes this takes time. Sometimes that elapsed time and the waiting love of the one who forgives will lead to the all-important discovery: It is not the deed, the word or the attitude that is so awful, but what has happened to the relationship, what attack has been made on the covenant. Biblical faith was unique in the ancient world in interpreting sin as a breach in a personal relationship with a living God. The biblical understanding of marital sin in all of its forms takes this same point of reference: What does this do to our covenant relationship? So costly grace does not pretend that nothing has happened. It waits for interior work to be done in the sinner's soul, a work that is deeper than remorse (the feeling of sorrow that one has been found out or that hard consequences are being experienced). Full forgiveness cannot be given until there is repentance, and repentance is that fruit of the Spirit which allows us to see our deed or attitude from God's point of view. It hates sin so much that it turns decisively from it. It is at that point that forgiveness becomes especially creative.

Creating a new future is part of forgiveness. Jesus said to the woman caught in adultery, "Go now and leave your life of sin" (Jn 8:11). Forgiveness neither condones nor condemns. On the strength of Christ's finished work on the cross, it shows *compassion*; we *feel (-passion)* the hurt of it *with (com-)* the one who hurt, bearing the pain of it and taking it to Jesus who alone can bear it fully. That gives us permission to work constructively for a new future.

Forgiveness, like healing, takes time. But it can hardly have its gracious impact if there is no confession. Lewis Smedes says:

To forgive is to put down your 50-pound pack after a 10-mile climb up a mountain.

To forgive is to fall into a chair after a 15-mile marathon.

To forgive is to set a prisoner free and discover that the prisoner was you.

To forgive is to reach back into your hurting past and recreate it in your memory so that you can begin again.

To forgive is to dance to the beat of God's forgiving heart.

It is to ride the crest of love's strongest wave.

Our only escape from history's cruel unfairness, our only passage to the future's creative possibilities, is the miracle of forgiving.[1]

Eucharist: The Creative Context for Confession

I said earlier that confession is to marriage what baptism is to the Christian life. There is, however, an important difference. Baptism is a once-for-all act, while confession is constantly repeated by couples determined to keep short accounts with God and with each other. Therefore I recommend as part of the marital discipline of confession the occasional practice of couple Eucharist. Eucharist, or communion, was meant to be a day-by-day vehicle for realizing the grace of Christ in our lives.

The Eucharist addresses three besetting sins in a marriage: pharisaism, possessiveness and power-hunger. Confronted with the visible signs of grace in the bread and wine, we are compelled to renounce our pharisaism. This is one table to which we dare not come thinking, "I am better than you." The ground is absolutely level when standing before the cross of Christ. We are also compelled to confess and renounce our possessiveness. Love so amazing, so divine, love that demands our all, makes a prior claim on our hearts. My petty demands, my claim on my spouse's time, affection and attention, the justification of my rights and my righteousness all pale before the acted parable that calls me to justify God rather than myself. For the God who reveals himself through crib and cross gives everything he demands, including righteousness. The Eucharist confronts power as well. The hunger for power even in the intimate politics of marriage is confronted by the dramatic parable of Christ's powerlessness on the cross. We choose the way of hierarchy, of control, either overtly or covertly. He chose the way of downward mobility. As we eat and drink the fruits of his powerlessness, we are both empowered to live his life of sacrificial love and persuaded to empower others rather than to overpower them. So it is appropriate that most liturgies of the Eucharist include a confession of sin and words that assure pardon. The table evokes confession and bestows forgiveness. What a good thing for a couple to come to give thanks at the communion table together!

I was heartened to find at least one writer on spiritual disciplines who confesses to the value of couple Eucharists, or breaking bread together. Morton Kelsey says this: "My wife and I discovered that our very different individual practice of private prayer can come together and reinforce each other at a daily Eucharist."[2] In his case it was part of the daily discipline of a small group that practiced the inner journey together. Many couples could avail themselves of the daily Eucharist provided by such groups or by some local churches. But here we'll explore the possibility of occasionally breaking bread as a couple.

In its original context the Lord's Supper was not only a meal, but a *family* meal. We have taken it away from the dining-room table and placed it in the sanctuary, with the sacred and the sacerdotal. In my opinion we have made it less, rather than more, sacramental by doing this. In the marriage sacrament, the partners are the celebrants, and the best place to celebrate is in the kitchen and the bedroom, not behind the altar! Catholic authors Evelyn and James Whitehead hint at the value of a home Eucharist but their tradition would be stretched to the breaking point if they were positively to propose it.

Protestants claim they have bound their conscience to the Word of God and subject every tradition to the liberating scrutiny of Scripture. Why not this one too?

The Bible says nothing about an ordained minister performing or officiating at this sacrament, or doing this in the context of a worship service. What the Bible does say is that we must discern our real relationships to the body of Christ (the church), to the body of Christ on the cross, and to the brothers and sisters who are the immediate body of Christ to us, lest we "eat and drink judgment" on ourselves (1 Cor 11:29). Two believing marital partners, perhaps including their believing children, are better able to remember Jesus with thanksgiving *(eucharisto)*, having confessed their sins to each other and living in fellowship, than a crowd of anonymous worshipers. At church we often stare at row after row of the backs of each other's heads, while the elements are distributed to people who do not even know each other well enough to be "out of fellowship."

Enjoying communion together can consist of the simple reading of 1 Corinthians 11:17-26 or Matthew 26:17-30, a prayer of thanksgiving, the breaking and sharing of some bread and the drinking of a common cup. These may serve as powerful means of grace in the home.

Celebrating Forgiveness

In a perceptive analysis of human sexuality Jean Vanier notes that forgiveness signifies and acknowledges the covenant with another. Because a man and woman belong to each other irrevocably, they are called daily to welcome each other just as they are with all their flaws. Being in covenant means that one has a reason to understand that "all the blockages, all the aggressive acts come, in great measure, from inner sufferings, anguish, and fears."[3]

Because the covenant is a sacred sign, an icon, God meets the couple in the act of forgiveness. Vanier asserts that the life of a married couple "is founded on this forgiveness which alone can heal the wounds inflicted on their unity. The road to unity must pass through daily forgiveness. And celebration, which is a sign that forgiveness is total, culminates in the tenderness and union of love. This union of love in spirit and body drives out all aggression and the blockages which might remain, and makes the two one flesh, one heart, one spirit." Then in his most daring metaphor, Vanier suggests that as a couple matures in confession and forgiveness, the sexual embrace is the communion service. "The union becomes eucharistic, an act of thanksgiving for having refound unity."[4]

In the grace of confession and forgiveness we can truly say, "This is my body broken for you," and hear Christ say the same to us.

Putting It into Practice

In *Married For Good* I proposed that the Ten Commandments are lifestyle statements for the covenant people. They also form an excellent outline of the obligations persons have in a marriage covenant. As an exercise in confession, take the following abbreviated meditation and walk through it individually, pondering and reflecting on each statement. I have added an "amendment" to each commandment to help us think about some of the emotional and spiritual loopholes we use to evade our full responsibility to our covenant partner. When you have completed the meditation, confess your faults and sins first to God. Then at an appropriate time confess them to your spouse. You may wish to seal your mutual confession and forgiveness by celebrating the Lord's Supper together.

The Ten Commandments and Our Amendments

1. You shall give exclusive loyalty to your spouse (after your loyalty to God) *unless it conflicts with your absolute duty to yourself to be a fulfilled person.*

2. You shall not make false images of your spouse but shall be truthful and honest *unless clinging to a false image or a past image of my spouse justifies my not working on the relationship.*

3. You shall honor your spouse's name in public and private

provided your spouse honors you.

4. You shall give your spouse time, rest and worth-ship *when it does not conflict with other priorities.*

5. You shall be rightly related to your own and your spouse's parents *if they do not make any unreasonable demands.*

6. You shall not destroy each other with hatred, destructive anger and uncontrolled emotions *unless provoked.*

7. You shall be sexually faithful and must control your appetites *unless your inalienable right to complete sexual satisfaction is not respected by your covenant partner.*

8. You shall not steal but rather live in community of property *unless having separate assets would make you more independent when you split up.*

9. You shall only speak the truth *unless telling the truth about an affair will destroy the marriage.*

10. You shall not covet any other spouse and you should be content with the spouse you have *but a little flirtation is adult play.*

From these amendments *may the Good Lord deliver us!*

For the keeping of the Lord's covenant obligations, *may the Lord equip us!*[5]

MUTUAL SUBMISSION: REVERSING THE CURSE

10

*D*URING OUR SIX YEARS OF MARRIAGE, WE TRIED TO develop our spiritual relationship. Time after time we fumbled and gave up soon after we started. The root problem was how each of us perceived spiritual leadership. I believed it was the husband's responsibility to initiate and maintain all spiritual disciplines for the family, while Earl held a more biblical perspective. I refused to explore his point of view and demanded to have spiritual disciplines observed in the way I expected."

As Louise tells the story of her marriage to Earl, she now discerns that a crucial impediment to their spiritual intimacy was actually *political* in nature. She required her husband to be the spiritual leader, believing that being "head" meant being "in charge of" the wife, or having power over the wife. As an educated, strong woman, however, Louise admitted that her idea of leadership was a conflicting mix of egalitarian values and chain-of-command assumptions. Earl's view of spiritual leadership had to do with *priority* rather than rulership. When he didn't lead the way she required, Louise misunderstood Earl's leadership as weak. By discovering the discipline of mutual submission, they eventually found a new harmony. Here is how Louise describes the process.

Earl reacted to my expectations by doing exactly the opposite as a protest to my demands. The struggle went on until I learned the biblical emphasis of spiritual leadership through the course on "Building Strong Marriages in the Local Church." Then I realized I should feed on Christ and his word for myself. It leaves no ground for me to slack off and blame it on my spouse for not setting an example "as a leader should."

I am accountable to God for my own spirituality and relationship to him. This prompts me to be responsible for my own spiritual state and turn to God directly for forgiveness and strength. Now that I know that it is permitted for the wife to take the lead sometimes, I can better appreciate the unique contribution that my husband gives. I can pray for my spouse and minister to him no matter what his spiritual condition is. I have discovered that I should never compare my husband's spirituality with mine. Pharisaism only produces self-righteousness and rots one's life from within.

With misconceptions of spiritual leadership cleared out of the way, I was more ready to confront some of the hindrances to intimacy in spiritual friendship. Like a newborn babe, I had to learn anew how to cherish Earl, how to communicate and keep short accounts of wrongs being done. And this is happening because we learned mutual submission.

I see Earl and Louise's story repeated time and again. Misunderstood spiritual leadership and failure to submit *mutually* prevent spiritual intimacy. That is why this is such an important discipline for couples. Spiritual friendship either finds an equal or makes one! One cannot have deep fellowship with a subordinate or a superior. But what does the Bible actually teach?

The Headship Bugaboo

In marriage the headship debate has everything to do with spirituality because it affects how we understand the position that each spouse has in Christ, and how Christ as head of the home leads a marital couple. In my view an unbiblical and unhealthy headship is one in which the husband is the spiritual authority of the home, and the wife is dependent on her husband's spirituality. It is really a marital offense, because it robs both husband and wife of the privilege of being priests to each other and co-priests to their family.

In my book *Married for Good*, I developed the biblical idea of headship carefully. Here only a summary can be given, but that chapter, "The Problem of Headship," can serve as a guide for any who want a more in-depth study of this issue. "The husband is the head of the wife as Christ is the head of the church" (Eph 5:23) is *mis*understood as meaning control, power, decision-making authority, ownership and accountability to God for one's wife and children. When the husband controls and the wife complies, God's heart breaks because neither husband nor wife is free to be real.

The hierarchical view of God-over-the-husband-over-the-wife-over-the-children has done inestimable harm to the spiritual health of wives and children, and (if they could only realize it) to husbands as well. Perhaps the husbands lose the most, because they have the truly impossible task of being the spiritual head of the home.

But in reaction to the chain-of-command headship, many Christians throw out headship altogether, leaving roleless, interchangeable marriage partners who want to be just spouses, neither husband nor wife. They have correctly emphasized mutual submission, but they have stripped marriage of its mystery by failing to honor the headship principle. There *is* a biblical balance, a place where both marital health and spiritual health can grow. *This biblical balance is headship within a covenant of equal partners, living out the mystery of Christ's relationship to the church.*

In a covenant of equal partners, a husband's headship means a priority in responsibility for the relationship in nurturing (loving), initiation, protecting and providing. Each couple must work this out in their own way. In *Married For Good* I compared Christian marriage with a drama for which we are given the plot line and the ending but the actors must write their own lines. This means we have no reproducible formula for the roles of husband and wife. Indeed, they are not roles at all, but the way each individual couple responds to their uniqueness and their calling to live out the drama of bride and groom, the drama of Christ and the church.

Complementarity means husband and wife are equal but different; different but one; one yet each still unique; and indeed their uniqueness is more apparent because they are together. One way that this uniqueness is seen is that both husband and wife bring distinct spiritualities to the relationship. The priesthood of all believers—male and female—means no less (Acts 2:17-18; 1 Pet 2:9).

If both men and women are priests in Christ, then the husband cannot be the exclusive priest of the marriage or family. It is a tragic anachronism to call a husband "the spiritual head" of the marriage.

The hinge verse of the marriage passage in Ephesians 5:21-33 is verse 21: "Submit to one another out of reverence for Christ." The husband's loving service (v. 25) and the wife's respect (v. 33) are simply appropriate ways for *each* to submit to the other. In a remarkable way this reverses the curse that has haunted the relationship of the sexes since the first pair.

The Reversed Curse

Originally the man and woman were side-by-side companions in the Garden (Gen 2:18-25). There is nothing in the creation story that suggests inequality or subordination. But once they sinned, God told them what consequences they would experience. To Eve, God said, "Your husband . . . will rule over you" (3:16). He also told Eve, "your desire will be for your husband" (3:16), not meaning the positive desire of sexual attraction but the negative desire to overthrow her master.[1] Rule and revolt is *not* what God wants between the sexes, but the inevitable consequence of separation from God. But in Christ, instead of *ruling* his wife, the husband *loves* her to death. Instead of revolting against her domestic master, the wife is free to bombard him with respect. This is not what each deserves. It is not even the duty each has to the other. It is gospel freedom, sheer grace. For one spouse to lay down his or her agenda and expectations before the other and to adjust, is a marital sign of the presence of Christ. The age of Christ has come.

How tragic it would be for Christians to base the politics of marriage on the curse, rather than on Calvary grace. Yet this is exactly what I see many believers doing. By missing the grace of mutual submission, they reduce spiritual intimacy. They miss one path to God in their marriage.

Married in Christ

The key to understanding the marriage section of Ephesians 5 is the emphasis on Christ. We submit to one another, Paul says, "out of reverence for Christ" (v. 21). Wives are called to submit to their husbands "as to the Lord" (v. 22). All of these relationships—mutual submission, servant headship and reverence—are *in Christ. They are not roles but expressions of spirituality.* Our life together in Christ is not based simply on mutual submission or on a male-female hierarchy, but on Christ who chooses to dwell in the covenant.

Dietrich Bonhoeffer showed the importance of this in *The Cost of Discipleship* when he explained that those who follow Jesus no longer have direct, immediate relationships with other persons.[2] Our most immediate relationship is with Christ, our divine mediator between God and humanity, and between people. Paradoxically, we get closer to others when we go through Christ. He delivers our relationships from the fleshly sins of control and compliance and frees us to be really present. Because of Christ's unconditional welcome, we are able to turn our hostility into hospitality.

But the emphasis of the Ephesians passage is not so much on loving our spouse through Christ, as loving Christ through our spouse. When we love Christ in and through a spouse, we are free to respond to Christ in our relationship, rather than responding directly to the treatment we receive from our spouse. For example, the husband has no headship authority in himself. Headship comes in Christ—period. And the wife has freedom to reverence her husband, not because of her husband's splendid character, or even the role he plays in her life, but because he is her husband *in the Lord.*

Mutual submission is the key not because it takes politics out of marriage by requiring each to lay down rights, but because mutual submission is our "reverence for Christ" (v. 21). We worship Christ our marital mediator in the context of the specifics of our lives together. We are one in Christ literally, not metaphorically. Jack Dominian was referring to this when he said, "What needs to be appreciated is that the moment-to-moment exchange between members of a family is prayer in the sense that they are addressing Christ in each other."[3]

This is especially true when we cope with our differences. Submission is not the same as capitulating or merely complying. Compliance is an adaption to a painful situation. Usually compliance leaves a person with a sliver of resentment. But submission is positive. It is putting ourselves under another, welcoming and receiving that person, adapting to his or her uniqueness.

Submitting to Our Differences
The discipline of mutual submission enabled Rob and Sue to welcome each other and to celebrate rather than blur their differences. Instead of being a political contest or a cold-hearted truce, their marriage became a daily prayer to God as they practiced the discipline of mutual submission.

Both Rob and Sue had found new life in Christ at the age of sixty. Rob was a technologist facing retirement at sixty-five. Sue had given most of her life to homemaking and raising four children. Perhaps it was the experience of the empty nest and forced retirement that prodded them both to hunger for more reality with God. At the time, they were elders of a lifeless church. Then Sue was struck with cancer.

Healing came for Sue as she wrestled with cancer surgery and also through the healing prayer of godly women she met. But Sue gained more than a clear bill of health. She now had a day-by-day living relationship with God. It was at this point that Sue and Rob found their way into a small, lively church. Sue found a new freedom in prayer and occasionally found herself speaking in another language, a prayer language that brought a new depth to her private devotional life. Her cancer healing opened many doors of ministry with the physically sick, and eventually she expanded her ministry to include inner healing or prayer counseling. Rob began to think that his wife was a little "touched," but he tolerated these new things as long as he did not have to become like her. But that was the problem.

Rob could welcome Sue's spirituality, but Sue could not welcome Rob's. From her point of view, Rob was a dour Scot that needed liberating. He was too rational, too calculating, too analytical and too empirical to pray for healing the way she did. "After all," he said, "most people you pray for don't get healed." Sue found Rob too calculating about the people that were being attracted to their church, like bees to honey. Sue saw these people as healed, renewed, saved and established. What Rob saw was men and women who needed to find a job, settle down and get their act together.

Unfortunately, neither Rob nor Sue realized how much they needed each other. She hoped Rob would take spiritual leadership in the home and initiate morning prayer and Bible reading as a couple. Now with the kids gone, they had no excuse. But Rob seemed to be more interested in the morning newspaper. Sue felt all she got from Rob were bits and pieces of his spiritual life, and not many at that.

Rob and Sue's story reveals a crucial area of mutual submission: *welcoming your spouse's spirituality.* The permutations and combinations of spirituality in marriages are as endless and various as there are human personalities, because God designed each person to be unique. No matter how well courted, adapted, adjusted and compatible two people feel before marriage, they will be struck, sometimes staggered, by the differences they discover in each other.

■ One may be more spiritually "alive" in the morning than the other. Think of what this does to the task of finding a time to pray together, or to the problem of choosing a late-night counseling ministry. One may be half asleep while the other is wide awake!

■ One may be an action-oriented person like Peter who wanted Jesus to invite him to walk on the water. The other might be more reflective, intuitive and meditative, like Nathaniel, whom Jesus saw meditating under the fig tree. Try long-range planning for ministry goals with that combo!

■ One may be expressive and spontaneous while the other is inward, thoughtful and calculating in spiritual matters. The former wants to light a fire under the latter; the latter wants the former to think before acting.

■ One leads from the heart. The other leads from the head. And each may find the other an impediment to doing things the "right" way.

■ One is a planner and is future-oriented. The other lives for the moment and believes that planning restricts the leading of the Spirit.

■ One is a people-person and finds the greatest spiritual pleasure in the company of like-minded believers and in caring for needy people. Solitude holds no magnetism for that person, while the other thrives on being alone.

■ One is drawn to evangelism as the best way to express kingdom ministry. This person doesn't need to be told to witness. It is as natural as falling off a log. But the other feels compelled to other kingdom priorities like the social and political structures of our society.

■ One loves to go to charismatic prayer meetings where there are tongues and interpretations, prophecies and words of knowledge. The other feels this is a dangerous diversion from the really important things of loving the last, the least and the lost.

There is a wide spectrum of spiritual gifts which will be expressed unevenly throughout the body of Christ—including our spouses. Mutual submission is not mutual capitulation but the grace of a mutual welcome. It means saying to a spouse, "I like you the way you are. I like what God does through you. I like the way you serve God. And I need you."

Years later Sue told me that she did come one day to welcoming Rob just as he was, rejoicing in his unique gift as a Christian. "When I stopped demanding that he become the spiritual leader of the home, as I thought he should," she confessed, "I suddenly realized that he was just what I needed as a leader." At this point Rob said, "And then I felt a new freedom to give myself spiritually to Sue even though I did not think (and still don't think) of myself as a spiritual leader. She is more advanced in Christ than I am, but then maybe we are just different. At least now we know that we need each other."

Mutual submission not only makes good marriage sense. It is a path to God. It is a sign to the world that Christ has reversed the curse. It makes living together everyday a gospel experience.

White Martyrdom

When Gail and I visited the Wedding Church in Cana of Galilee, we told the resident Roman Catholic clergyman, Brother Joseph, an Italian, that we were celebrating our twenty-fifth anniversary. "Mama mia," he said, "twenty-five years of martyrdom!" Then we introduced Gail's mom and dad who had just celebrated their fiftieth. "Mama mia," he gasped once again, "a fifty-year martyrdom!" We laughed with him uproariously, knowing he was right. In marriage, death and life interpenetrate, as crucifixion and resurrection are eternally joined. Married persons are literally buried into each other, physically, emotionally and spiritually, losing themselves but finding themselves in the other. Both the physical and the spiritual have their counterparts in this mutual burial and resurrection.

Some people refuse to do this and remain as married singles or terminally unmarried. The Orthodox Church has always understood that marriage was such a path of joyful martyrdom. In their ceremony, the bride and groom receive crowns of leaves and flowers, or of precious metals. The crowns are crowns of joy but they are also crowns of martyrdom for no true marriage succeeds without self-sacrifice and spiritual passion.

In a seventh-century Celtic homily there is a deep reflection on the forms that martyrdom may take. Red martyrdom is losing one's life in a violent death for the sake of Christ. Green martyrdom is the path of asceticism, denying one's bodily appetites in a kind of living death. But there is a third kind of martyrdom that comes closest to the purpose of this book. White martyrdom is the path by which we place love for Christ above all other competing loves.[4]

Our ten couple disciplines are simply ways to love God more, through and alongside our spouses. Happily, this also leads us to

a deeper love for our spouses. In all of its earthiness and everyday-
ness marriage is a main highway to God, never a detour. It is a form
of dying to self through which we come alive.

May you and your beloved wear your martyr's crowns well together!

Putting It into Practice

The following inventory has helped many couples identify the areas
where they are having difficulty in submitting to one another, or
where they are complying instead of submitting. In your marriage,
whose responsibility do you think it usually is now to make decisions in each of the following areas? Answer by drawing a circle
around the appropriate alternative. Use one color for the husband
and another for the wife.

	Almost Always Husband		Shared Equally		Almost Always Wife	Does Not Apply
a. Where couple lives	1	2	3	4	5	-
b. What job husband takes	1	2	3	4	5	-
c. How many hours husband works	1	2	3	4	5	-
d. Whether wife works	1	2	3	4	5	-
e. What job wife takes	1	2	3	4	5	-
f. How many hours wife works	1	2	3	4	5	-
g. Number of children in family	1	2	3	4	5	-
h. When to praise or punish children	1	2	3	4	5	-

i. How much time to spend with children	1	2	3	4	5	-
j. When to have social contact with friends	1	2	3	4	5	-
k. When to have social contacts with in-laws and relatives	1	2	3	4	5	-
l. When to have sex	1	2	3	4	5	-
m. How to have sex	1	2	3	4	5	-
n. How to spend money	1	2	3	4	5	-
o. How and when to pursue personal interests	1	2	3	4	5	-
p. Whether and, if so, which church to attend[5]	1	2	3	4	5	-

Now look back over the way in which you think decisions are now made in your marriage. Use an X to indicate how you think decisions *should be made* in your marriage.

The areas where there is a discrepancy between what is and what ought to be are important things to discuss. But after you have discussed them, and what changes you would like to make, why not pray? The discipline of mutual submission calls for an almost impossible degree of self-giving between two centers of decision making. The stronghold of the will must be assaulted by love, not only the love of our spouse, but the ultimate Lover. Therefore this is a path to God, nor merely a technique of marital decision making. It is a prayer for an interior transformation. Mutual submission, to the extent that we have experienced it, is a sign that God is already finding us. It is a relational sign and wonder, an indication that we have already been touched by God's grace. As Mike Mason says, in his classic on marital spirituality, marriage is "a monasticism in which the vow and discipline of chastity becomes the vow and discipline of fidelity, in which the vow of poverty is translated into an unqualified sharing of the totality of one's life and possessions, in which the vow of stability applies not to a place or a fraternity but to a particular person, and in which the vow of obedience is practiced not in community but in partnership, and not to a superior but to an equal."[6]

Notes

Beginning the Journey
[1]Paul Tournier, *To Understand Each Other* (Atlanta: John Knox Press, 1968), p. 20.

[2]In *Married For Good* (Downers Grove, Ill.: InterVarsity Press, 1986), I defend a "headship" model that presumes the priority of the husband but eliminates headship as rule.

[3]Henri Nouwen, *Reaching Out: The Three Movements of the Spiritual Life* (Garden City, N.Y.: Doubleday, 1975), p. 72.

[4]These three dimensions are outlined in Kenneth Leech, *Soul Friend: The Practice of Christian Spirituality* (San Francisco: Harper and Row, 1977), p. 123.

[5]William Law, *A Serious Call to a Devout and Holy Life* (London: Epworth Press, 1961; first published, 1728), p. 8.

[6]Dolores Leckey, *The Ordinary Way: A Family Spirituality* (New York: Crossroads, 1982), p. 17.

[7]My working definition of spirituality is *making intentional the development of our relationship with God through Christ as a response to his grace in the totality of our lives.* Each word points to the need for marriage spirituality: *intentional* (it takes definite, repeated and persistent decisions to live under God's direction), *development* (it is an ongoing process over many years), *relationship* (the heart of it is belonging to God through the New Covenant in Christ), *response* (God is seeking us in our marriage more than we are seeking him), *grace* (spirituality is not the ascent of the human spirit to God like an eagle, but the gracious descent of God's Spirit like a dove to meet us in the reality of our lives), *totality* (spirituality embraces vocation, relationships, work, home, leisure, community and justice in society), *life* (because God's goal is not to make us religious but to enable us to live for the praise of his glory [Eph 1:6, 12, 14] in the entirety of our bodily existence).

[8]Morton T. Kelsey, *Companions on the Inner Way* (New York: Crossroads, 1985), p. xii.

Chapter 1: Prayer: Sharing a Special Intimacy
[1]Gene O'Brien and Judith Tate O'Brien, *Couples Praying: A Special Intimacy* (New York: Paulist Press, 1986), p. 93.

²Ibid., p. 13.
³ Richard F. Lovelace, *Dynamics of Spiritual Life* (Downers Grove, Ill.: InterVarsity Press, 1979), p. 88.
⁴Ibid., p. 90.
⁵As with most of the personal illustrations in this book (except those from my own marriage), this one is a collage of several people, well disguised. Some persons, however, have requested that their stories be printed verbatim, but with changed names.
⁶Tertullian, "Ad Uxorem," quoted in Kenneth Stevenson, *Nuptial Blessing: A Study in Christian Marriage Rites* (New York: Oxford University Press, 1983), p. 17.
⁷Lovelace, *Dynamics of Spiritual Life*, p. 159.
⁸Quoted in ibid., p. 160.
⁹O'Brien, *Couples Praying*, p. 14.
¹⁰Lovelace, *Dynamics of Spiritual Life*, p. 155.
¹¹Jack Dominian makes a fascinating conjecture that the reason for Sarah's five marriages was her inability to consummate, which modern counselors understand in terms of anxiety toward the act of sexual intercourse. If this is true, the sensitivity and gentleness expressed in Tobias's prayer might be the reason she was able to overcome her difficulties in allowing the consummation of her marriage to him. See Jack Dominian, *Marriage, Faith and Love* (London: Dalton, Longman and Todd, 1981), pp. 239-40.

Chapter 2: Conversation: Listening to the Heart
¹Tilden Edwards, *Spiritual Friend* (New York: Paulist Press, 1980), p. 48; cited in Leckey, *Ordinary Way*, p. 30.
²Aelred of Rievaulx, *Spiritual Friendship*, trans. Mary Eugenia Laker (Kalamazoo, Mich.: Cistercian Publications, 1974), p. 63.
³Ibid., p. 115.
⁴Ibid., p. 76.
⁵These questions are adapted from two other lists: some were supplied by Roberta Hestenes during a course she taught while at Fuller Seminary, and some come from Francis Vanderwall, *Spiritual Direction* (New York: Paulist Press, 1981), p. 74.

Chapter 3: Sabbath: Playing Heaven Together
¹Lynn M. Foerster, "Spiritual Practices and Marital Adjustment in Lay Church Members and Graduate Theology Students" (Ph.D. dissertation, Graduate School of Psychology, Fuller Theological Seminary, Pasadena, California, 1984). Using a fine-tuned questionnaire with 247 Christian laypersons, she evaluated

both the extent of their experience of high marital satisfaction and their practice
of common spiritual life, the subject of this book. The particular dimensions of
common spirituality she measured were, in order of importance, prayer with
spouse, experiencing the presence of God while praying with one's spouse,
experiencing communion with one's spouse while praying, engaging in a time
of quiet or "setting oneself apart from the world," and experiencing God's presence during church worship. She found a high level of correlation between
shared spiritual discipline and good marital adjustment, at least among the
young, childless couples she surveyed.

[2]Leckey, *Ordinary Way*, p. 17.
[3]Henri Nouwen, *The Genesee Diary: Report from a Trappist Monastery* (Garden
City, N.Y.: Image Books, 1976), p. 41.
[4]Madeleine L'Engle, *Walking On Water: Reflections on Faith and Art* (New York:
Bantam, 1980), p. 98.
[5]See Hugo Rahner, *Man at Play* (New York: Herder and Herder, 1972).
[6]Michael Quoist, *Prayers* (Fairway, Kans.: Andrews and McMeel, 1974), p. 98.

Chapter 4: Retreat: Sharing Solitude
[1]Nouwen, *Genesee Diary*, p. 48.

Chapter 5: Study: Hearing God Speak Together
[1]You may obtain a copy of McCheyne's Calendar for Daily Readings from The
Banner of Truth Trust, P.O. Box 621, Carlisle, PA 17013, U.S.A.

Chapter 6: Service: Full Partnership in Ministry
[1]Aelred, *Spiritual Friendship*, p. 63.
[2]See also Kenneth C. Russell, "Marriage and the Contemplative Life," *Spiritual
Life* 24, no. 1 (Spring 1978): 48-57.
[3]Cited in Janet Morley, "In God's Image?" *New Blackfriars* 63, no. 747 (1982):
375; quoted in Kenneth Leech, *Experiencing God: Theology as Spirituality* (San
Francisco: Harper and Row, 1985), p. 374.
[4]On this, see Bruce Waltke, "The Relationship of the Sexes in the Bible," *Crux*
19, no. 3 (September 1983): 10-16.
[5]For example, Donald and Inge Broverman, "Sex Stereotypes and Clinical Judg-
ments of Mental Health," *Journal of Consulting and Clinical Psychology* 34
(1970): 1-7.
[6]Søren Kierkegaard, *Sickness unto Death* (Garden City, N.Y.: Doubleday, 1954),
p. 183.
[7]Nouwen, *Genesee Diary*, p. 80.
[8]Ibid., p. 81.

[9]Nor Hall, "Feminine Spirituality," in *Westminster Dictionary of Christian Spirituality*, ed. Gordon S. Wakefield (Philadelphia: Westminster Press, 1983), pp. 148-50.

[10]Harriet Ziegler, "Female View Important to Theology," in *Canvas*, no. 9, World Council of Churches Sixth Assembly, Vancouver, Canada, August 4, 1983, p. 1.

[11]Hall, "Feminine Spirituality," p. 149.

[12]There is a fascinating rabbinic discussion of the male Jewish prayer thanking God that one has not been made a non-Jew, a slave or a woman, in Rabbi Hayim Haley Donin, *To Pray As a Jew: A Guide to the Prayer Book and the Synagogue Service* (New York: Basic Books, 1980) pp. 196-97. A partial quote of his argument follows:

> Some may interpret this blessing as a grudging resignation to a lesser state, or as the acceptance of one's fate. But Rabbi Aaron Soloveitchik, a leading contemporary Talmudic scholar, views it as a blessing that affirms woman's innate superiority over man. It is God's wish, he says, that human beings achieve the Divine qualities of compassion and mercy. Woman is naturally closer to that level of perfection than is man. She was given the gift of mercy and compassion. Is not God Himself addressed as *Rahum*, the Compassionate One? And is not *rehem*, the Hebrew word for womb (the part of the body that more than any other distinguishes woman from man and symbolizes her essence) a form of the same word that means compassion? A woman can therefore proudly claim to have been fashioned "according to His will."
>
> Man, on the other hand, cannot make the same claim. Although given the gift of power and strength to conquer the earth and subdue it, man lacks the natural qualities by which he may achieve the spiritual ideal. He starts with a baser nature than does woman, and is therefore in need of greater refinement. Since *mitzvot* are seen as a means of purifying a person's soul and perfecting his character, man needs to keep more *mitzvot* because he has further to go toward the ideal.

[13]See Leech, *Experiencing God*, pp. 350-78.

[14]Ibid., pp. 353, 366.

[15]Jean Vanier, *Man and Woman He Made Them* (Toronto: Anglican Book Centre, 1985), p. 57.

[16]1 Corinthians 11 deals with an urgent problem: maintaining sexual distinctiveness or, as we have called it, a sexual spirituality. The problems Paul dealt with in his letters to Corinth were related to the revolutionary impact of the liberation of women in Christ. The Jewish women came out from the back of the synagogue where they had remained silent. Now they were praying and prophesying in the meeting. But some of them, apparently taking their freedom too far, took off their veils when they came to church. Culturally, the veil was then, as it is

today in the Middle East, a sign of submission to a husband, a sign of femininity, a matter of decent and proper dress for a woman. It would have made the church an object of public scandal if the women did not wear their veils. Today it would be like women and men taking off their wedding rings as they came into church, saying, in effect, "In Christ there is neither male nor female . . . and it's just as though we were not married."

Paul gives a carefully and finely tuned argument to deal with liberation gone too far. This passage speaks a vital word for us today at the point of our modern sexual confusion. While in Christ there is neither male nor female, with respect to acceptance—just as there is no Jew or Greek, no bond or free—*in Christ we become more male and more female than our society might ever imagine.*

If Paul had wanted to say men were over women generally he could have said just that in 1 Corinthians 11:3, or at least he could have grouped the various orders in the hierarchy one after another: God is head over Christ who is head over man who is head over woman—as a chain of command. Instead of listing them as an order of hierarchies, Paul is *comparing relationships.* And his use of the word *head* here implies "source" rather than "ruler" or "chief." Later he speaks about how the man was the source of woman when God created Eve out of Adam. God is the source of Christ who proceeded and came forth from the Father, as Christ is the source of any man's life in God, as man is the source of woman.

Radical Christian feminists demolish headship because so many Christian men have interpreted headship as rule. Their wives, although they thought they were submitting, were actually complying, and resentment often seethed within them. But headship is beautiful. It means there is order in God's world and even order within God himself. While it is heresy to say Jesus is not equal with God the Father, there is a kind of priority of the Father over Jesus, a priority with equality. Headship has nothing to do with inequality or inferiority. It is a *priority in a relationship of equals,* a priority which Paul develops in Ephesians 5 as a priority in protecting, nourishing, loving and sacrificing. Androgyny and hierarchy are not the only options—full male-female interdependence and partnership must be considered.

Kathleen M. Galvin and Bernard J. Brommel, *Family Communication: Cohesion and Change* (London: Scott, Foresman and Co., 1986), pp. 104-5, represents the current trend in psychology toward supporting androgyny, the capacity for members of both sexes to be masculine and feminine in their behaviors— both dominant and submissive, active and passive, tough and tender. They cite a considerable body of literature which supports that androgynous married partners demonstrate more understanding of their spouses because they concentrate on communication behaviors rather than maintaining sex stereotypes.

A moderately androgynous viewpoint is taken by John A. Sanford, *The Invisible Partners: How the Male and Female in Each of Us Affects Our Relationships* (New York: Paulist Press, 1980). A more radical viewpoint is taken by Phyllis Trible, *God and the Rhetoric of Sexuality* (Philadelphia: Fortress Press, 1978).
[17]Vanier, *Man and Woman*, p. 54.

Chapter 7: Sexual Fasting: The Discipline Nobody Wants
[1]*Ketuboth* 5.6-7 in Herbert Danby, *The Mishnah: Translated from the Hebrew with Introduction and Brief Explanatory Notes* (Oxford: Oxford University Press, 1933), p. 252.
[2]Gordon Fee, *The First Epistle to the Corinthians* (Grand Rapids, Mich.: Eerdmans, 1988), pp. 266-83.
[3]Pope John Paul II, *Apostolic Exhortation of His Holiness: The Role of the Christian Family in the Modern World* (St. Paul Editions, 1981), pp. 29-30.
[4]Fee, *First Epistle to the Corinthians*, p. 280.
[5]Vanier, *Man and Woman*, pp. 127-28.
[6]Evelyn Eaton Whitehead and James D. Whitehead, *Marrying Well: Possibilities in Christian Marriage Today* (Garden City, N.Y.: Doubleday, 1981), p. 13.
[7]See Russell, "Marriage and the Contemplative Life," pp. 48-57.

Chapter 8: Obedience: Doing God's Will Together
[1]This story is told in chapter one of R. Paul Stevens, *Liberating the Laity: Equipping All the Saints for Ministry* (Downers Grove, Ill.: InterVarsity Press, 1985).
[2]There are a few notable exceptions.

Chapter 9: Confession: The Surgery of Forgiveness
[1]Lewis Smedes, "Forgiveness: The Power to Change the Past," *Christianity Today* 27, no. 1 (7 January 1983): 22-26.
[2]Kelsey, *Companions on the Inner Way*, p. 112.
[3]Vanier, *Man and Woman*, pp. 127-28.
[4]Ibid.
[5]Paul Stevens, *Married for Good: The Lost Art of Staying Happily Married* (Downers Grove, Ill.: InterVarsity Press, 1986), p. 87.

Chapter 10: Mutual Submission: Reversing the Curse
[1]The same Hebrew word for *desire* is used for the negative desire of sin to overmaster Cain in Genesis 4:7.
[2]Dietrich Bonhoeffer, *The Cost of Discipleship* (London: SCM Press, 1959), p. 85.
[3]Dominian, *Marriage, Faith and Love*, p. 262.

[4]J. Ryan, *Irish Monasticism* (London, 1931), p. 197.

[5]These questions are found in the "Marital Pre-Counselling Inventory" used by The Counselling Group of Burnaby Christian Fellowship, Burnaby, B.C.

[6]Mike Mason, *The Mystery of Marriage* (Portland: Multnomah, 1985), pp. 142-43.

Printed in the United States
134923LV00002B/61/A